GYM CLIMBING
Improve Technique, Movement, and Performance

MOUNTAINEERS
OUTDOOR EXPERT
series

GYM CLIMBING
Improve Technique, Movement, and Performance

Matt Burbach
Photography by Jon Glassberg

Second edition

MOUNTAINEERS
BOOKS

MOUNTAINEERS BOOKS is the publishing division of The Mountaineers, an organization founded in 1906 and dedicated to the exploration, preservation, and enjoyment of outdoor and wilderness areas.

1001 SW Klickitat Way, Suite 201, Seattle, WA 98134
800-553-4453, www.mountaineersbooks.org

Printed in China
Distributed in the United Kingdom by Cordee, www.cordee.co.uk

First edition, 2004. Second edition, 2018.

Copyeditor: Erin Cusick
Design: Mountaineers Books
Layout: Peggy Egerdahl
All photographs by Jon Glassberg, Louder Than Eleven, www.lt11.com, unless noted otherwise
Cover photograph: *Emily Harrington focused and determined at Earth Treks Climbing Center, Golden, Colorado*
Frontispiece: *Matt Segal mid-bouldering season with Emily Harrington spotting*

Library of Congress Cataloging-in-Publication Data
Names: Burbach, Matt, author. | Glassberg, Jon, photographer.
Title: Gym Climbing : Improve Technique, Movement, and Performance / Matt
    Burbach ; Photographs by Jon Glassberg.
Description: Second edition. | Seattle, WA : Mountaineers Books, [2018] |
    Includes bibliographical references and index.
Identifiers: LCCN 2017058660| ISBN 9781680511420 (pbk) |
    ISBN 9781680511437 (ebook)
Subjects: LCSH: Indoor rock climbing. | Climbing gyms.
Classification: LCC GV200.2 .B86 2018 | DDC 796.522/4--dc23
LC record available at https://lccn.loc.gov/2017058660

Mountaineers Books titles may be purchased for corporate, educational, or other promotional sales, and our authors are available for a wide range of events. For information on special discounts or booking an author, contact our customer service at 800-553-4453 or mbooks @mountaineersbooks.org.

Printed on FSC®-certified materials

ISBN (paperback): 978-1-68051-142-0
ISBN (ebook): 978-1-68051-143-7

Contents

Introduction.. 7

How to Use This Book 11

CHAPTER 1

Gym Climbing

Evolution of Climbing Gyms.. 18

Disciplines of Gym Climbing.. 18

The Modern Climbing Gym 21

What to Expect 26

CHAPTER 2

Equipment

The Essential Items... 30

Gear Considerations 45

Purchasing Equipment.. 48

CHAPTER 3

Movement Technique

Weight Shifting.. 54

Footwork.. 58

Body Positioning 63

Hand Grips 66

Matching Hands and Feet 70

Crossing Through 75

Dynamic Movement... 80

Sequencing.. 85

CHAPTER 4

Bouldering

Getting Started 89

Safety.. 91

Following a Problem 91

Hitting the Ground 93

Advanced Techniques 98

CHAPTER 5

Top-Rope Climbing

Getting Started 110

Grades... 111

Tying In 112

Belaying.. 116

Communication.. 126

Putting the System Together 129

Auto-Belay Systems... 131

Closing the Loop 132

CHAPTER 6

Lead Climbing

Getting Started 135

Responsibilities of a Lead Climber 136

Responsibilities of a Lead Belayer................................ 151

Putting the System Together 160

Following a Lead Route.. 163

CHAPTER 7

Performance

Technical Skill.. 167

Mental Approach... 168

Physical Conditioning 174

Scheduling and Periodization 193

Competitions... 197

Maintaining Balance.. 201

Beyond the Gym 203

Acknowledgments 207

Resources 208

Glossary... 209

Index 216

Opposite: *Gym climbing is as much a mental activity as it is a physical one.*

Introduction

When George Mallory, a 1920s mountaineer obsessed with being the first person to summit Mount Everest, was asked what motivated him, he said, "Because it's there"—a simple answer driven by his desire to explore. But why we climb is often much more complex than that. Using your hands and feet in the vertical world connects you to the environment in a new way, and strong friendships and bonds frequently form through the experience of sharing a rope with a climbing partner. For some, climbing is an excuse to travel the world and experience the outdoors from a vertical perspective. Looking out from the top of a crag or cliff that you can get to only by climbing is priceless. Climbing something that looks, or is, unclimbable on your first attempt is a test in mental and physical fortitude that leads to self-satisfaction. Climbing can be enjoyed for many reasons, and there are multiple ways to be involved in this discipline.

Climbing participation is best represented as a pyramid. At the top are high-altitude alpinism and mountaineering,

attracting those who set their sights on summits like Mount Everest or remote peaks in Patagonia. This type of dedication, high level of experience, and acceptance of risk represents a small fraction of climbers. Below the tip of the pyramid are pursuits like ice climbing, trad climbing, sport climbing, top-roping, and bouldering—all forms of outdoor climbing. But at the bottom of the pyramid, with the highest number of participants, lowest commitment required, and fewer barriers to entry, gym climbing makes up the foundation. Aspiring climbers, in any discipline, will most likely be introduced to the activity through a climbing gym.

Founded in Seattle more than thirty years ago, the Vertical World climbing gym was the first to move the traditionally outdoor sport of rock climbing into an indoor arena. Now, millions of people around the world have discovered the physical and mental challenges and rewards, as well as the great social setting, of indoor climbing. At the time of this second edition's publication, there are approximately five hundred commercial climbing gyms throughout the United States, together forming a multi-million-dollar industry. Every state in the nation has an indoor climbing facility, with many cities boasting several gyms. For example, both the Denver metro area and San Francisco Bay Area have a dozen commercial gyms. In addition, several hundred universities, colleges, and fitness centers have also constructed artificial climbing walls for recreation and fitness.

Anyone who has tried or seen climbing knows inherently that hanging fifty feet in the air by a rope held by a partner should not be taken lightly. Climbing safely requires practice and knowledge, which in turn requires solid, clear instruction in all of the necessary skills. While climbing groups, clubs, and even "teams" are becoming more popular, learning the ins and outs of climbing beyond the basics is usually an exercise in both apprenticeship and self-instruction.

To support this unique and exciting learning process, Mountaineers Books presents *Gym Climbing: Improve Technique, Movement, and Performance*, a manual for novices just entering the sport of indoor climbing as well as for more-experienced climbers who want to improve their technique, strength, endurance, or knowledge of indoor safety systems. *Gym Climbing* responds to a demand by indoor climbers for a complete reference, one that reflects the fact that gym climbing has evolved from a foul-weather alternative to outdoor climbing into a sport in itself, complete with its own vocabulary, techniques, skills,

and culture. This reference supports both novice and experienced climbers in mastering the art and science of gym climbing. Recent consumer insight research suggests that about two-thirds of all climbers in the United States climb primarily in gyms. These numbers demonstrate a huge shift from ten years ago, when the average climbing gym member used it as a place to train and stay in shape for rock climbing outdoors.

New climbers will value *Gym Climbing* for its broad and deep treatment of all aspects of indoor rock climbing, including everything from information on gear investment choices to details on proper top-rope systems management and movement technique. A beginner will not need another reference for indoor climbing skills and techniques because this book grows with the climber. As the user of *Gym Climbing* masters skills and techniques, he or she will be ready to move on to the more advanced skills covered, like indoor lead climbing and belaying.

More advanced indoor climbers will appreciate chapters on topics such as lead climbing indoors and performance. With easy access to gyms, experienced outdoor climbers are now climbing indoors. As this advanced crowd will tell you, there is no better way to develop climbing strength, technique, and endurance than actually climbing, and gym climbing allows for maximum training in minimal time. *Gym Climbing* presents a comprehensive set of techniques and training exercises. All exercises described have been used by thousands of climbers coached by the author, and the author has taken the experiences of those climbers to improve upon and adapt the exercises as needed. Outdoor traditionalists will also find this book helpful because, even for veteran rock climbers, the indoor approach to belay skills, movement technique, and training can leave an outdoor climber lost in an indoor world. This book will facilitate the transition from climbing on real rock to pulling on plastic.

Finally, although this book is designed as a complete reference for the indoor climber, mastering the skills presented is not a substitute for sound judgment, experience, and personal and group instruction. Ultimately, every climber is responsible for his or her safety in this activity, where participants face risks that are inherent to the sport of climbing. *Gym Climbing* does not prepare a climber to take on the challenges of climbing outside on real rock. For guidance on climbing outdoors, pick up a copy of *Rock Climbing: Mastering Basic Skills* from Mountaineers Books; for the second edition, Topher Donahue updated Craig Luebben's reliable how-to manual.

How to Use This Book

The contents of *Gym Climbing* are organized to reflect the climbing learning process, beginning with an overview of indoor climbing facilities and then moving on to discuss equipment. The fundamentals of climbing movement and technique are similar across all disciplines of gym climbing, so this topic covers bouldering (climbing low to the ground, unroped), top-roping (climbing on ropes attached to preset anchors), and lead climbing (setting the anchor as you climb up). It wraps up with performance improvement. Reading this book from cover to cover may instantly gratify the enthusiastic learner, but gradually working through and mastering the skills described in each chapter is the most effective way to ensure safe and steady improvement. As your climbing skills and ability develop, review past sections before moving forward to keep from forming bad habits, which we all know are very hard to break.

Body positioning and technique will improve your chances on overhanging boulder problems.

KEY EXERCISES

Throughout the book, key exercises provide all readers an opportunity to either practice and master skills before progressing or revisit those skills that they need to improve. For example, you wouldn't want to practice sky diving by jumping out of a plane. Instead, practicing the fundamental skills in a controlled environment will help you tackle this complicated, complex activity. The same is true for gym climbing, where the consequence for climbers is meeting the force of gravity head-on.

Gym Climbing presents key exercises that promote the development of specific skills required for safe climbing and belaying in an indoor climbing environment. Covering everything from top-rope belaying to bouldering techniques, these exercises are designed to break the greater picture of climbing into smaller, more manageable pieces. Practicing these exercises also allows the reader to identify personal strengths and weaknesses and to build confidence before applying these skills in a "live" climbing situation.

All of the key exercises were performed at Earth Treks Climbing Center in Golden, Colorado. An indoor climbing facility with a strong focus on instruction, Earth Treks designed a climbing area for teaching, complete with skill practice areas equipped with anchors, carabiners, bolts, and holds needed for specific exercises. Even if your gym does not have gear or holds established for you to practice the key exercises, performing them should still be quick and easy with a little imagination. Climbing gyms want climbers to be safe and make progress, so helping you set up key exercise areas is in their best interest. Other than some technique skills, all key exercises are designed to be performed near the ground.

A NOTE ABOUT SAFETY

Safety is an important concern in all outdoor activities. No book can alert you to every hazard or anticipate the limitations of every reader. The descriptions of techniques and procedures in this book are intended to provide general information. This is not a complete text on climbing technique. Nothing substitutes for formal instruction, routine practice, and plenty of experience. When you follow any of the procedures described here, you assume responsibility for your own safety. Use this book as a general guide to further your knowledge. Under normal conditions, excursions into the backcountry require attention to traffic, road and trail conditions, weather, terrain, the capabilities of your party, and other factors. Keeping informed on current conditions and exercising common sense are the keys to a safe, enjoyable outing.

—*Mountaineers Books*

Without climbing gyms, Matt Segal, who grew up in Florida, never would have been introduced to climbing.

Emily Harrington's career as a professional climber started with competitive gym climbing.

THE PROS

The professional climbers depicted in many of the photos throughout the book are Emily Harrington and Matt Segal. The two of them have put in the time, dedication, and practice to enable themselves to push the envelope of climbing in their respective disciplines. While Matt and Emily set their sights, goals, and aspirations on rock climbing in places like Yosemite or remote walls of China, or sport climbs in Rifle, Colorado, they still have a symbiotic relationship with gyms. At home or on the road, gyms are their training hub allowing them to work on their own climbing weaknesses and develop their strengths, even though they're already expert performers.

Matt got his start climbing in Florida, where the local gym was his only option. As soon as he could, he moved to Colorado's Front Range to be closer to rock. He had set his sights on hard traditional climbing, putting up difficult routes and first ascents at the 5.14 grade, one of the most difficult levels. For Matt, who's also an international traveler, climbing and adventure are synonymous.

Emily is a five-time National Sport Climbing Champion who has evolved into an all-around climber at the upper echelons of the sport. She has completed multiple first female ascents of 5.14 routes, summited Mount Everest, and free climbed Yosemite's El Capitan. A well-rounded mountain athlete, Emily constantly pushes her personal boundaries of exploration.

Opposite: *Climbing gyms are the center of climbing culture in urban areas.*

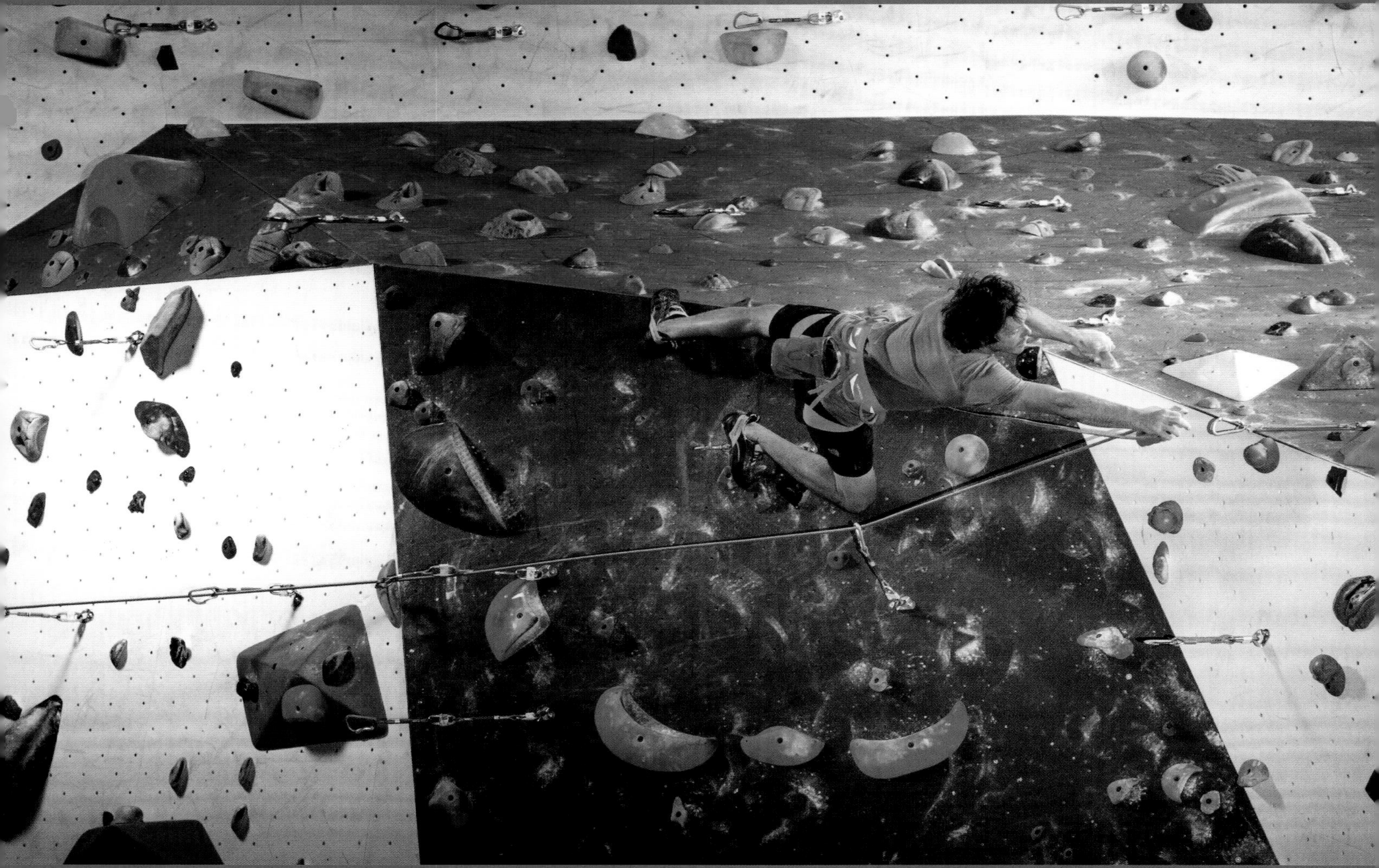

CHAPTER 1

Gym Climbing

People of different abilities and ages can enjoy this unique activity together. Climbing takes us out of our normal horizontal world and into a physically demanding and mentally challenging vertical environment. Some climbers choose to reach high peaks of the world, like the summit of Mount Everest. Others enjoy climbing at local rock faces after work with their friends. And still others choose to ascend frozen waterfalls. The avenues of climbing are extremely varied, each with its own environment, set of technical skills, and physical demands.

Gym climbing—climbing on fabricated climbing-wall structures—is the fastest growing aspect of climbing in terms of participation and locations. There are more than five hundred indoor climbing gyms in the United States, with plenty more in Europe, and those numbers are rising. Ask gym climbers why they choose to climb indoors, and a typical response is "because it's fun." The attraction stems from the physical, mental, and even social benefits that gym climbing provides.

Indoor climbing challenges both the body and the mind. Although climbing may be perceived as an upper-body-intensive activity that requires (or develops) broad shoulders and sturdy forearms, every major muscle group in the body contributes to climbing's physical demands. Even with proper technique, tough climbs can leave your whole body sore the next day. The full-body aspect of climbing not only develops muscle stabilization and increases strength, but also can improve your joint flexibility and range of motion. And the physical aspect of climbing is just the tip of the iceberg.

Climbing is as much a cerebral activity as it is physical. The excitement comes from the problem-solving skills needed to figure out a particular movement and then actually complete that move. You have to anticipate what hold you want to grab next or how to shift your weight over your feet. Climbing demands complete focus on the task at hand, clearing the mind of daily distractions.

The climbing gym can bring professionals and novice climbers together—or in the case of the pair shown here (Emily and Matt), perhaps two professionals.

Although your own power and decision-making determine your success on a particular route, gym climbing is an incredibly social activity. To climb on a rope, you need a partner to ensure your safety. To boulder near the ground without a rope, you often need spotters to help control your fall. Whatever the type of climbing, your partners can motivate you and make the activity more enjoyable. These bonds last far longer than the duration of your climb. Climbing is an activity where elite performers and beginners can participate with each other. Everyone in the climbing gym has something in common: their appreciation of climbing.

For someone interested in rock climbing, starting in a gym is a logical first step. The technical skills of gym climbing are transferable to climbing outdoors. For most people, gyms are more accessible than outdoor destinations. It may be impossible to go rock climbing after work or school, but a gym allows for easy access and enjoyment. Another appeal of indoor climbing is the control of the environment. Devoid of bugs, falling rocks, storms, sweltering heat, snow, darkness, or steep approaches, gyms provide a more comfortable environment for those who may be less inclined to pursue climbing outdoors.

EVOLUTION OF CLIMBING GYMS

Rock climbing outside is weather dependent. Sunny, warm days generally offer the best conditions, and the wetter and colder it is, the more dangerous the conditions. Even with perfect weather, you cannot rock climb without access to rocks. Climbers without access to natural rock turned to alternate faces, like stone buildings or the underside of bridges.

Walls built specifically for climbing first emerged in Europe in the 1960s. These basic outdoor structures resembled brick walls with holds chipped out and glued-on pieces of rock. While these outdoor structures provided a great climbing opportunity on pleasant days, inclement weather rendered them useless. Rock climbers looking for a way to train for climbing on stone used these walls. Outdoor walls are still popular in Europe; most of the international climbing competitions are held at outdoor venues to allow for maximum spectator attendance.

In the late 1980s, indoor climbing walls started popping up in the United States. Rather than mimic the real rock appearance of outdoor structures, handholds were molded into more tendon-friendly and comfortable shapes. Such holds allowed climbers to train longer and avoid injury. In addition, the indoor environment allowed climbers to train at any time of the day and in any season. While commercially inclusive to all audiences, these gyms were built by climbers for climbers. The shift to climbing indoors also lowered barriers to entry for the sport. Beginning in the 1990s, an entire population of climbers learned to climb indoors at these gyms.

Climbing gyms experienced a fundamental shift the following decade. While seasoned climbers would tolerate dark, dusty (and occasionally smelly) gyms, these places weren't particularly attractive to someone having their first climbing experience. As the climbing lifestyle grew in popularity, gyms focused on becoming hubs for the existing community and also creating an inviting atmosphere for novices. Gyms became the home base of a community that values fitness and health.

DISCIPLINES OF GYM CLIMBING

Within climbing gyms, there are different disciplines. Just like ski resorts that offer different types of terrain for subsets of skiing (groomers, park and pipe, sidecountry, etc.), climbing gyms offer a few different ways for people to enjoy the sport

Without ropes and equipment, bouldering focuses on the pure movement of climbing.

indoors. These different types of climbing can be enjoyed outside as well.

BOULDERING

A few decades ago, rock climbers scrambled over boulders to get to rock faces. Today, climbing on these refrigerator- to building-sized boulders is a sport in its own right. Characterized as difficult unroped climbing, bouldering usually takes place relatively close to the ground, although some extrem-ists push the envelope with high ascents, known as highballs. Boulderers protect themselves from high-speed impacts with the ground by landing on padded mats and using spotters, similar to what gymnasts do. Climbing gyms have designated bouldering areas, without top-rope or lead climbs set above them. Because it does not require rope work, bouldering offers the lowest barrier to entry to gym climbing. There are a handful of bouldering-only gyms, as a space's height requirement is much lower than that of a top-rope or lead climbing gym.

The security of a rope running from the climber to the top of the climb and back down to the belayer makes top-roping the most popular form of roped climbing.

TOP-ROPING

When most people think of climbing, top-rope climbing usually comes to mind. With this style of climbing, the climber ties in to the end of a rope that is already attached to an anchor at the top of the climb and runs back down to the belayer standing on the ground. The belayer is the climber's partner who minimizes the slack in the rope between the two of them as the climber ascends the wall. If the climber falls or wants to weight the rope, the belayer secures the rope to keep it from slipping. The belayer is also responsible for lowering the climber back to the ground. Top-roping is the most popular introduction to climbing.

LEAD CLIMBING

The limitation of top-roping outdoors is setting up an anchor at the top of the climb. When climbing a big rock wall or mountain, it is impossible to secure the first climber with a top rope, since getting to the top is the adventure's objective! In these instances, the climber ascends with the rope trailing down to the belayer. The belayer feeds rope out to the climber as he or she goes up. To protect the climber from hitting the ground after a fall, the lead climber places pieces of protective hardware into the rock and clips the rope to them. In the event of a fall, the climber falls past the last piece of protective gear until the rope is pulled taut. For safety reasons, gyms use fixed bolts for lead climbers to clip the rope into. Lead climbing and belaying are the most technically and mentally demanding forms of gym climbing,

Emily secures the rope to the wall as she lead climbs.

since the consequences of a fall are more serious than in top-roping.

THE MODERN CLIMBING GYM

Most major cities offer some sort of gym climbing facility. If your options are limited, then you will simply climb at the nearest gym. If you are fortunate enough to have several options, know that not all gyms are created equal. The most common question is how tall are the walls? Though this may seem like the most important issue to a new climber, climbers have different needs in a gym. The novice climber may look for one with a reputation for offering great instructional classes. In contrast, an elite outdoor climber might look for a gym with great route setting, overhanging walls, and a fitness area for training purposes. A boulderer may prefer a bouldering-only gym.

SIZE

A handful of climbing gyms have walls taller than fifty feet, but most gym walls are between twenty-five and fifty feet tall. Less than thirty feet makes for short routes, but that is enough for new climbers. Currently, the tallest artificial climbing wall in the United States is 165 feet (on the side of a building), but tall indoor walls are fifty feet and higher. Often, gyms express the total amount of wall space in square feet. However, this figure does not give you any information about the layout of the facility, how tall the walls are, or even how much of it is really climbable. Gyms with more than 25,000 square feet of climbing surface are considered large by industry standards.

ROUTE SETTING

Climbing gyms have specific paths, or routes, established by a route setter. The holds on the wall are made of a plastic resin

It's never too early to start climbing. Most gyms have youth programs, both recreational and competitive.

and have a bolt hole through the middle, allowing the route setter to reposition the holds. For the most part, the routes are set with specific movements in mind. More difficult climbs typically involve intricate and complex movements. Since route setters have their own distinct styles of setting, a good route-setting team will ensure some variety in the style of routes to climb. A well-rounded gym has a wide selection of routes, from easy ladder-like climbs for beginners and children to challenging test pieces for elite climbers. Routes are identified with tape or holds that are the same color. Each route is rated in terms of relative difficulty, using the Yosemite Decimal System (YDS), bouldering V scale, or a rating system that the gym has devised itself.

Route setting has evolved over the past decade. Initially, the movement on indoor routes mimicked movement found outside on real rock. But with the popularity of bouldering and spectator-friendly competitions, route setting has become more dynamic and the climbing less straightforward.

HANDS-ON INSTRUCTION

While instructional literature (like this book) serves as a reference for climbing skills and techniques, hands-on instruction from a qualified professional is essential for safety and continued progress. Sure, your buddy can "show you the ropes," but how do you know he is a competent and safe climber? Even a "really good climber" may not necessarily be able to verbalize the nuances of body positioning or advanced technical skills. Beginners are not the only group of climbers who can benefit from instruction. At any stage of your climbing career, there is always more to learn, and an instructor can help advance your skills.

Indoor climbing schools vary greatly. Some have weekly classes and programs, while others offer only private instruction. If possible, get an insider's feel for the climbing school's classes by asking other climbers about their experiences. Find out where the class is held, since learning how to belay or boulder in a crowded area with climbers not in your class can be hectic and can detract from your learning. Ask the gym staff about the ratio of students per instructor, total number of students in the class, and frequency of classes to see what is right for you. More than six students per instructor for any type of climbing class can be difficult to manage.

Find out what type of training the instructors receive before being able to teach classes. The quality of an indoor climbing school is only as good as its instructors. Do not be afraid to ask for the best instructor to suit your needs, even for group classes. Sometimes classes are free for gym members, while other times they charge a fee, depending on the instructors and specialty of the class.

YOUTH TEAMS AND PROGRAMS

Gym climbers are all ages, but kids take to climbing like monkeys take to trees. Children's small size and fearless attitudes make no climb too challenging to try. To accommodate the growing number of young climbers, most gyms have children-specific courses and programs. Gyms have youth programs, from birthday parties and summer camps to recreational and competitive junior teams. Check for times that an instructor is available to belay for children. For kids who want more than an opportunity to climb, look for youth programs that teach more advanced skills like belaying or climbing technique.

Because yoga and climbing share similar mental and physical attributes, it's not uncommon for gyms to have a yoga studio and offer classes.

Participation in junior climbing teams has reached an all-time high, as most gyms support a youth climbing team. Not all teams share the same values, though. Some may have tryouts and stringent training schedules planned around the competition season, with an intensity similar to many gymnastics teams. Other teams simply create an environment that allows young people to climb with each other on a regular basis with little emphasis on competition, either within the group or against other teams.

NOT JUST CLIMBING

Climbing gym owners are well aware that their member base is built of people who value the fitness and well-being that climbing provides. Many climbing gyms take their tie to health and fitness one step further by offering nonclimbing-related services and facilities. General fitness and strength-training facilities are common, as well as climbing-specific training areas. Studios are also quite common, with gyms offering yoga, Pilates, and other group classes. Some gyms now have shared work spaces, Wi-Fi, massage and physical therapy services, saunas, steam rooms, cafés, and coffee bars.

CULTURE AND COMMUNITY

When so many people with a similar interest come together, their social interactions create culture. Climbing gyms have become the urban hubs of climbing culture. Many gyms recognize this important role and therefore organize events, volunteer opportunities to promote climbing stewardship, and social gatherings, and they host art shows and guest lecturers. Climbing is merely the shared experience that brings these people together, fostering lasting friendships.

INDOOR CLIMBING IN FITNESS CENTERS

Just as climbing gyms are adding components of overall physical fitness and health to their facilities, fitness centers are adding climbing walls. The growing

Fitness centers within climbing gyms allow for cross-training and full-body workouts.

Hangboards, system boards, and training walls make up climbing-specific training decks. You'll find the most-dedicated climbers here, deliberately improving their climbing

popularity of indoor climbing as a form of fitness has led traditional gyms to take steps like modifying racquetball courts to build climbing walls or adding treadmill-style climbing machines to satisfy their clients' desires to climb. Because climbing is not the primary focus of these establishments, a commercial climbing gym will better meet your needs. However, a few fitness centers have more-than-adequate climbing facilities.

Community centers and organizations such as the YMCA are also adding climbing walls to their facilities. Climbing promotes a healthy and active lifestyle, particularly among young people, and can help improve self-confidence and body and spatial awareness. Perhaps the largest institutional push to build climbing walls has come from colleges and universities. Newer recreation centers have included climbing walls in their designs, and older facilities have added artificial outdoor climbing walls. These walls are often part of outdoor recreation programs. Check on the availability of using climbing walls that do not belong to commercial gyms. Some of these facilities allow climbers to use their walls for a daily fee, even if you do not belong to the facility that owns them.

WHAT TO EXPECT

Each gym usually has several options for novices to get started. Not all gyms are set up to allow an individual to try climbing or receive instruction on a walk-in basis. If a gym has auto-belay systems (mechanical belay systems that do not require a belayer), they may be able to let you climb at any time. Check into open climbing times, during which an instructor is available to let you try a few climbs for a nominal fee. While noninstructional programs can get you started climbing, an introductory class gives you a better feel for the activity as a whole.

TAKING AN INTRODUCTORY CLASS

Climbing for the first time requires little instruction, but belaying competently requires a learned set of skills and sufficient practice applying them. Enrolling in an introductory class is the best way to start your climbing career. Usually, an introductory class teaches novices how to properly put on a safety harness, tie in to the rope as a climber, and belay, all while allowing for some time to climb. These skills are essential to any type of roped climbing you may pursue, inside or outside. Climbing shoes, a harness, and belay hardware are included with the class. The responsibilities of a belayer are serious, with potentially extreme consequences for mistakes. An introductory class prepares you to take (and hopefully pass) a belay competency test. Some gyms have packages that include an introductory course and limited free entry to the facility.

BELAY TEST

To manage liability and ensure member and visitor safety, gyms administer rather stringent belay tests. Before a gym allows a novice to belay unsupervised, you must

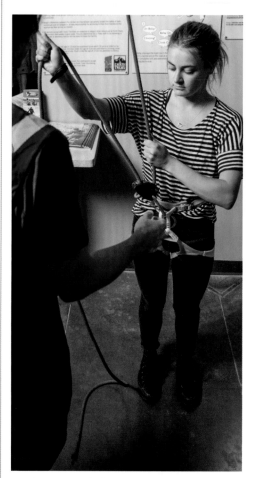

Passing a gym's belay test gives the gym (and you) the confidence that you can belay effectively.

take and pass a belay test. This practical exam shows the gym staff that you know the basic principles of how to use a harness, belay, and properly tie in to the rope as a climber. There is no set standard for this test across all gyms, but following the techniques and procedures in this book will adequately prepare you for any belay test. You will have to take each gym's belay test to be certified in that facility. Gyms test climbers for top-rope climbing and lead climbing separately, and all gyms have a minimum age requirement for belay testing. Since each gym sets its own standards, there is no national belay-test certification. Organizations like the American Alpine Club and Climbing Wall Association are working to establish national standards for belay certification.

WAIVER OF LIABILITY

Every gym requires participants to sign a waiver of liability before climbing or belaying. The most common public perception is that the waiver's sole purpose is to avoid litigation should an accident occur. But more importantly, signing the waiver acknowledges risk on behalf of the participant. It is in your best interest to read every word of the waiver, especially if you are a first-time climber. Some gyms even have you sign a helmet waiver if you choose to forego a helmet.

Climbing, just like driving your car or mountain biking, entails risk. A climbing gym has created an opportunity for you to climb, and by climbing at all, even in a gym, you are subjecting yourself to certain risks. Signing the waiver means that you understand and are aware of these risks and *choose*—despite the risks—to cling to a wall thirty feet up in the air. Ultimately, you are responsible for your own actions and safety. Think twice about gyms that do not require waivers or belay tests. Such actions are evidence that the gym does not take reasonable precautions to help create a safe climbing environment.

ENTRY OPTIONS

On average, expect to pay $15 to $30 for a day pass. Off-peak hours may be cheaper, like during a weekday afternoon. A day pass should allow you to leave and reenter the gym and is usually the only option for a day of climbing, regardless of how long you climb. Expect to pay rental fees on top of the entry fee. Shoes, a harness, and a belay device typically rent for $10 altogether. Most gyms offer bulk-rate day passes, like a punch card, or multiple visits at a cheaper rate. Monthly passes are a nice option if you are not going to climb indoors all year.

Gym memberships are usually the way to go if you plan to climb all year round at least once a week (climbing two or three times a week is common for gym climbers). Ranging anywhere from $45 to $75 a month, these memberships are similar to a fitness center membership. The fee allows you to climb whenever the gym (or multiple gyms) is open and may even give you extra perks such as free courses, guest passes, members' parties, yoga or fitness classes, or even gear or instruction discounts.

THE LIFESTYLE

Climbing, particularly gym climbing, has such a strong pull on its participants. It starts with the activity itself. The cerebral problem-solving to figure out a correct hand or foot sequence engages the mind. The physicality of executing those moves strengthens the body, and the gains are often visible. And the social network of like-minded people builds community. All these pillars of personal growth come together at the gym, and the most successful gyms embrace this and build communities through stronger individuals.

Once you start going to the gym, and particularly if you become a member, it will become a central hub in your life. You'll meet your friends at the gym after work to climb. Or by climbing after work, you'll meet new friends. Moving to a new city? Just visiting? The gym is a great place to start getting to know people and tap into the community. Stressful morning at work? A quick gym session at lunch can put your mind right for the rest of the day. Chances are pretty good that your relationship with gym climbing will evolve from an activity into a lifestyle.

Opposite: *Knowing how to use safety equipment is as important as knowing safety techniques.*

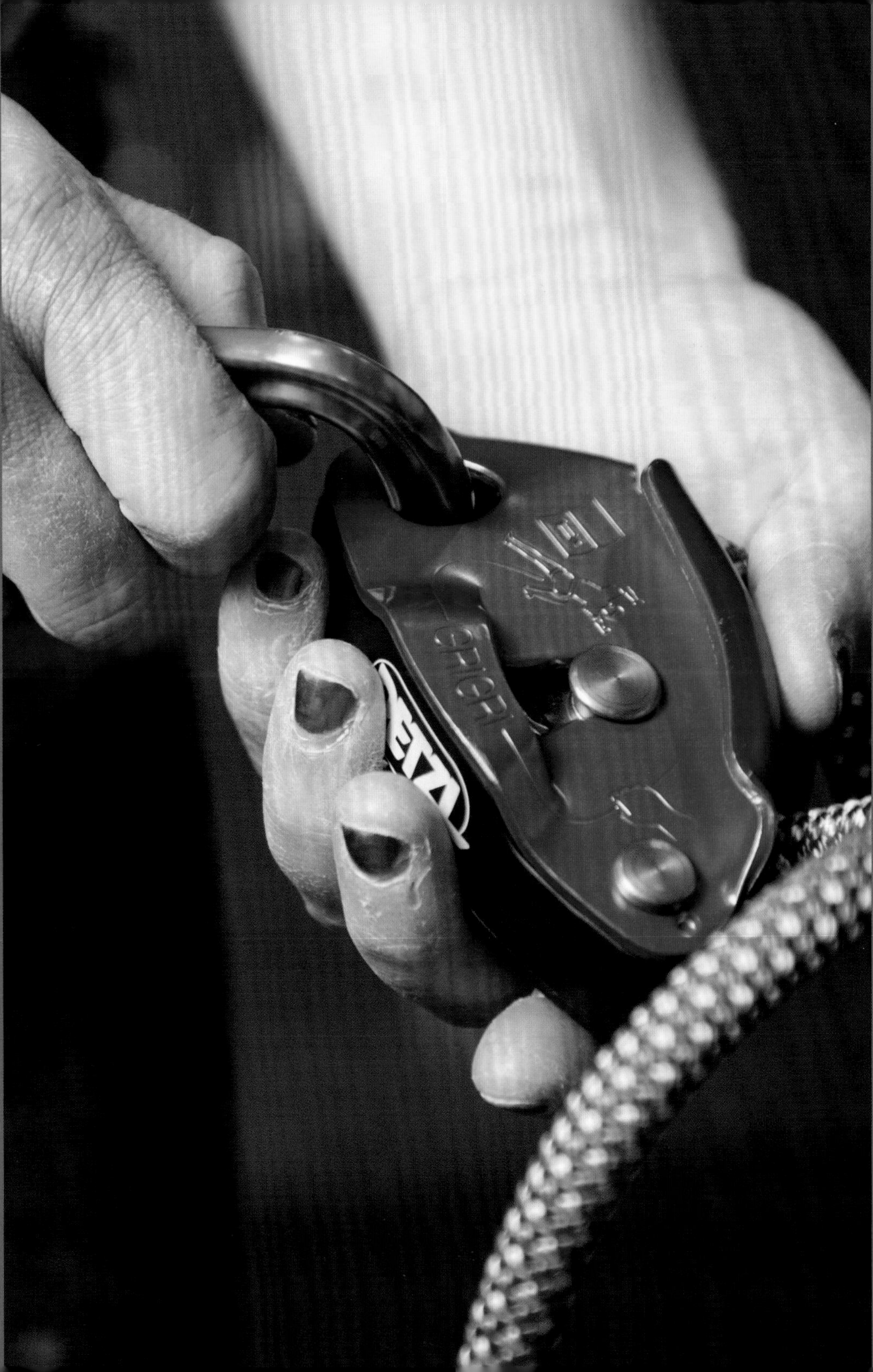

CHAPTER 2

Equipment

A love of climbing comes from the freedom of moving in a vertical environment. However, this freedom can position us dozens of feet off the ground in potentially dangerous situations. Climbing gear provides the link between staying safe and pushing your physical and mental limits. The rope attaches the climber and belayer to each other, harnesses attach the rope to the climber and the belayer, and carabiners attach the rope and belay device to the harnesses. Not only does this gear minimize the risk of injury, but it also enhances performance and makes climbing more enjoyable. Major recent developments in climbing gear have addressed comfort and functionality. Equipment and gear is constantly being made lighter, more comfortable, and stronger, and to many consumers, a lower price is always a plus.

THE ESSENTIAL ITEMS

To get started climbing, at minimum you will want a pair of climbing shoes. Although it is possible to climb in any shoes (or even barefoot), sticky-soled climbing shoes will make a huge difference in your performance. If you want to climb on a rope, you will also need a harness, belay device, and a locking carabiner. As your climbing career progresses, you may find that you need (or want) more specialized gear. Perhaps start by renting equipment at your local gym to decide what works best for you.

CLIMBING SHOES

Technically, you can climb in any shoes, just like you can run a marathon in flip-flops, but shoes affect your performance more than any other climbing gear (just like running shoes for the aforementioned marathon). Whether you boulder or climb ropes, shoes are the only piece of gear used in all disciplines. While a harness is the most important piece of safety gear that must be fitted to a climber, it minimally affects performance. Technological advances in shoes have significantly affected the evolution of rock climbing. With their sticky rubber and secure fit, they will make a difference in your climbing, too.

Last

The last is the constructed inner sole of the shoe. Gym and rock climbing shoes are constructed on a slip last. With this style, the shoe is constructed first, and then a last is slipped into the sole. The sensitivity of slip-lasted shoes is determined by the thickness and material of the midsole and the thickness of the shoe rubber. Last shape varies as much as foot shape varies.

Shape

The shape of the last is the shoe's "footprint" and contributes to overall fit and comfort. A straight last creates minimal torque on the foot and is the most comfortable. New climbers and someone wanting a shoe to wear all day will find a straight last desirable. The more curved the last, the more pressure and torque on the foot. Sharply downward-pointing toes improve performance on steep and technical terrain.

Rubber

No two climbing-shoe manufacturers use the same rubber compounds on their shoes. The differences are stickiness and durability. Softer rubber tends to be stickier but wears more quickly than harder, less sticky compounds. Some climbers may go through a lifetime of climbing and not be able to tell the difference between types of rubber, while others swear by one brand over another and even have brand-new shoes resoled with the rubber of their choice. Most shoes are constructed with four- to five-millimeter rubber soles, and high-performance shoes use rubber as thin as three millimeters for sensitivity. Thin rubber wears out faster than thicker soles.

Upper Material

The upper part of the shoe is made from either leather or synthetic materials. Leather is typically cheaper, stretches from prolonged use, and is highly durable. Synthetic uppers offer a soft, thin feel while minimizing stretch and maintaining durability. Most climbing-shoe manufacturers offer shoe models of either leather or synthetic uppers. Some shoes may have a combination of both materials. For instance, a synthetic toe box keeps the fit tight around the toes, and leather around the rest of the shoe opening provides a comfortable fit. Mesh fabrics are becoming more popular, too, due to breathability and comfort.

Lining

The shoe's upper material and lining (or lack of lining) determines the overall stretch of the shoe. The lining on the inside of the shoe is often a canvas or synthetic material. Lining a shoe can maximize comfort and feel while minimizing stretch. The stretch of an unlined shoe is at the mercy of the upper materials. An unlined synthetic upper may stretch as little as a lined leather upper. Unlined leather shoes stretch the most, as much as a full size after persistent use.

Style

There are three general styles of climbing shoes: slippers, Velcro, and lace-ups. They all have their place in climbing and some styles are more appropriate than others, depending on the terrain.

Slippers. Slippers are constructed without laces or a closure system. An extremely tight fit and elastic at the opening keep the shoe secure on the foot. Once the shoe is on, fit adjustments are impossible. If there are any loose spots in the shoe, there is no way to tighten them except to wear a smaller shoe. Because of the extremely tight fit, most climbers wear their slippers only while climbing and take them off while belaying or resting. The midsole of slippers is thin and soft (even nonexistent in some models), allowing maximum sensitivity. On steep terrain, with a soft slipper, you can actually curl your toes around footholds for maximum feel. This benefits experienced climbers who have developed the proper foot strength to use their feet efficiently.

Because of their minimalist construction, slippers are priced at the middle to lower end of the spectrum. However, inefficient footwork can quickly grind down the rubber and ruin a new pair of slippers.

Velcro. Velcro-closure shoes are a great compromise between the speed and ease of putting on a slipper and the support and fit of a lace-up shoe. The Velcro-closure straps make putting on the shoes a breeze and provide some fit adjustment once they are on. Some are extremely sensitive and soft, while others have more edging power. Some companies offer zipper-closure shoes instead of Velcro. Velcro-closure shoes are popular among gym and sport climbers because they blend sensitivity with fit and performance.

Lace-ups. Lace-up climbing shoes offer the most adjustability in fit. The lacing system extends all the way down to the toes, providing adjustment points throughout the entire shoe. Tightening or loosening the laces at different spots on the shoe provides the most exact fit of all the shoe styles. For the most part, lace-up shoes offer greater foot stability and a strong edging platform, imperative for small edges. Entry-level lace-ups are constructed to provide foot support and stability, as well as durability. For all-around climbing on varying terrain, lace-ups are an excellent option when buying your first shoe.

Use

Among the different styles of shoes, there are basically two spectrums of use, ranging from comfort to performance fit.

Comfort. Comfort shoes are suited for a new climber, or a climber who wants enough room in their shoes to wear them for extended periods of time. These shoes tend to be designed and constructed with more volume and a flat profile to allow the foot and toes to relax in the shoes. The additional room allows for a comfortable fit, while sacrificing footwork precision.

Performance. Performance shoes usually have a more aggressive design that pushes the toes forward and holds the foot in a more powerful position. The tightness allows for the precision needed to stand on and use tiny holds. Performance shoes may be soft and supple for maximum sensitivity or maintain a rigid edge for standing on micro-footholds.

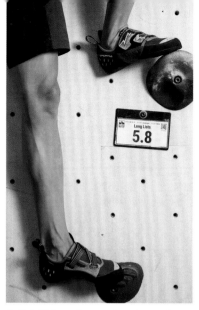

A flat, Velcro-closure shoe is great for comfort, and you can put them on and take them off quickly.

A flat lace-up allows for a more precise fit.

This shoe balances edging power and comfort, and offers lace-up adjustability.

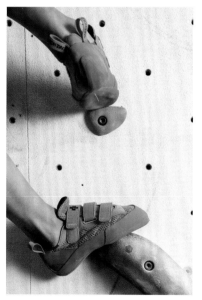

Three Velcro closures offer good fit, and a soft sole allows a climber greater sensitivity.

A molded heel cup creates a secure fit with powerful edge control.

A down-turned sole excels in steep terrain and allows for precise footwork.

Trying Shoes On

While research may help you narrow your choice of shoes down to a selected few, the most important criteria is fit. If possible, buy the actual shoe that you try on. Because of the handmade craftsmanship, there can be slight differences in fit, even with the same size shoe of the same model. Trying on shoes can be a tiresome process, but patience will get you the most out of your investment.

Climbing shoes are usually worn without socks. Wearing socks creates another barrier between your feet and the wall. This additional barrier makes your foot slide around while climbing and hinders sensitivity. To get your foot into the shoe, open the shoes up as much as possible. For slippers, fold the heel down to the sole to maximize the opening. Slide your foot all the way to the front of the shoe and use the heel tabs to slip the back of the shoe over your heel. For lace-ups, loosen the laces all the way down to the toe. Tighten the laces starting with the toes and work your way up to the ankle. There is no adjusting with slippers, and Velcro shoes offer minimal adjustments.

Shoe Fit

Climbing shoes should fit snugly but should not be overly tight or painful. Your toes should be at the end of the shoe with not much wiggle room. A snug fit alleviates sliding inside the shoe and allows for more precise footwork. However, if the shoes are painful, your attention will be focused on your feet, not the climbing. Look for an all-around snug fit, but avoid pressure points or loose spots. Also, excessive bunching of the upper material should be avoided. Your heel should be cradled by the shoe with limited dead space. In your search for a new shoe, take your time and be sure to try on shoes from different manufacturers. Some companies have reputations of fitting certain types of feet, but give several shoes a try.

The type of shoe also influences the fit. A slipper with a down-turned toe and radically curved last warrants a tight fit, with the knuckles of the toes buckled up and toe tips scrunched into the end of the shoe. A straight-lasted lace-up with a flat-foot design allows the toes to lie flat and just barely touch the front of the shoe. Wearing a loose slipper or a lace-up too tight limits the functionality of the shoe.

Consider the shoe's potential stretch. As mentioned before, this depends on the upper material, lining, and shoe size. Whoever helps you fit your shoes should be able to tell you how much a shoe stretches. The tighter a shoe fits, the more pressure is exerted on the uppers and the potential for stretching increases. A wall test is your best indicator of performance and fit, just like you would do when fitting a harness. Your climbing gear retailer should allow you to step on some holds to get a feel for the shoes. If that is not possible, step up and down on the edge of a bench or step to imitate climbing footwork and placement. Also, try to pull the shoe off your foot by hooking your heel on a hold or edge. The shoe should still be secure under this heel-hook test.

Women-specific shoes tend to have a lower volume and narrower heel.

Once you find the best-fitting shoe, take one more step to ensure it is the perfect-fitting shoe. Try the next size up and down so you know the size you choose is best suited for you. All these steps are necessary in buying shoes because they are not returnable once climbed in, and you do not want to be stuck with ill-fitting foot-wear. Use a climbing-shoe expert for advice and guidance, but ultimately the choice is yours. If you are uncertain about the sizing, you can always add socks to shoes that stretch too much, but if the shoes are too small, they are useless.

Gender-Specific Shoes

Women-specific shoes are designed to accommodate the shape and volume of women's feet. They're narrower and have less volume than their male or unisex counterparts. Some companies brand them as "low volume" shoes. If you have narrower feet, consider trying on a low volume or women-specific model.

Caring for Shoes

Wearing tight-fitting and nonbreathable shoes without socks and walking around barefoot before putting them on is less than

35

hygienic. Do not be the person your friends avoid when you pull your shoes out of your bag. Zap your shoes with antibacterial spray or powder after a climbing session and store them outside your bag so they can ventilate. The hot trunk of your car is not a good place for climbing gear.

If the insides of the shoes turn black from who knows what (it does happen), scrub them with a bit of mild detergent or soap, using a small brush. To protect the soles, avoid walking in dirt and dust. Clear the soles by scrubbing them with a wire brush and rubbing alcohol. Periodically check the soles for excessive wear.

Resoling

Eventually, the soles wear down, usually near the inside edge. It is a matter of when, not if. A climber with delicate and precise footwork may get a year of climbing out of a single pair without needing a resole; whereas the shoes of someone with "aggressive" footwork (loud foot placements and scraping or dragging the toes against the wall) may need doctoring after only a few months. Resoling saves your shoes and keeps you from having to purchase another pair. There are multiple mail-in climbing-shoe resolers, which are generally easy to find online or by asking climbing friends for references.

A brand-new pair of climbing shoes has an even seam where the sole of the shoe meets the thin rubber that comes up from the bottom on the sides and front (the rand). When this seam becomes jagged near the toe or the sole starts to delaminate

from the rand, send the shoes in for a half resole. The cobbler will replace that half of the sole with new rubber. The work of a skilled resoler will not affect the sizing or shape of your shoe. If you wait longer before resoling your shoes and wear into or through the toe rand, then a half sole and re-rand operation is necessary for resuscitation. Having a shoe re-randed often changes the shape of the toe box. If a hole wears past the rand to the leather, you are too late.

These shoes are due for a resole. Wait any longer, and they'll be irreparable.

HARNESS

When climbing with ropes, a harness is essential for safety and comfort. It is the attachment point between your body and the rope. Harnesses vary in adjustability, padding, materials, weight, and fit. An improperly fitting harness is not only uncomfortable, but potentially dangerous as well.

The most popular type of harness consists of a waist belt, leg loops, and a belay loop. Purchased in different sizes according to waist and leg circumference, these harnesses fit a wide range of body types. Full-body chest harnesses are appropriate for children too small to fit securely in a waist-belt harness. Women-specific harnesses are designed around female fit ratios of waist to leg size.

Waist Belt

The most comfortable harnesses have padding and wide webbing to disperse the climber's weight. Thoughtfully designed harnesses are wider across the back, where more pressure is created when the harness is weighted, and tapered toward the front to minimize bulk. Various types and layers of foam laid into the core of the waist belt provide padding. Synthetic lining on the inside can add comfort against the skin. Some companies use mesh fabrics or open cutouts in the back of the harness to keep the climber cooler in warm weather.

Harnesses have one or two buckles on the waist belt. A single buckle makes the harness slightly lighter and more streamlined. However, if a climber is in

A harness with adjustable leg loops allows for a wider range of fit around the legs.

Fixed, or nonadjustable, leg loops are more streamlined and less bulky than ones with buckles.

between waist-belt sizes, a harness with a single-buckle waist belt may mean that the center of the waist belt's back might not line up with the center of the climber's back. With two-buckle waist belts, tightening each buckle evenly allows the front and back of the waist belt to stay centered on the climber.

Leg Loops

Like the waist belt, the leg loops are padded for comfort. A harness will have either fixed leg loops or adjustable leg loops. Fixed leg loops are proportionally sized to the waist belt. For people who have narrow waists and sturdy thighs, for example, the buckles on adjustable leg loops allow for a wide range of leg size. The buckles are also helpful for providing a comfortable fit when layering with pants or shorts.

Belay Loop

The belay loop is a reinforced loop of webbing that attaches the waist belt to the leg loops. As the strongest part of the harness, the belay loop is the connection point to the belay device and floor anchors.

Gear Loops

Gym climbing harnesses should have at least one gear loop on each side so that your belay device and carabiners hang from the gear loops rather than dangling from your belay loop. Only inexpensive, entry-level, or rental harnesses do not have gear loops. Harnesses with four gear loops are common, but harnesses with up to six are designed for carrying the vast amounts of equipment needed for outdoor leading. Gear is more easily unclipped from rigid molded-plastic loops than from webbing surrounded by plastic tubing.

Rear Keeper Straps

The rear keeper straps attach the back of the leg loops to the back of the waist belt. Tightening these straps keeps the leg loops high on the thigh. Loose straps let the leg loops sag uncomfortably and limit range of leg motion. Detachable straps can be helpful in outdoor climbing but are not necessary indoors.

Buckles

At a minimum, a harness will have one buckle on the waist belt. Some may have up to four buckles (two on the waist belt and one on each leg). Keep in mind that multiple buckles add minor weight and bulk to your harness. Regardless of how many buckles the harness has and where they are located, they must be securely locked before use. A few manufacturers use self-locking buckles, but the standard buckle must be manually doubled back for security.

Harness Fit

Proper fit isn't just for comfort, it's also for safety. Too big, and you could potentially slide out of your harness if you turn upside down. Too tight, and your movement is restricted.

Waist. When fitting your harness, compare your waist size to the manufacturer's sizing chart. This will give you a

The waist belt should be pulled snug around the narrowest part of the waist: a, loose buckle; b, tight buckle. Follow the manufacturer's instructions to properly lock the buckles.

good indication of harness size, but you should still try it on. Stepping through the leg loops, pull them up as high on your thighs as is comfortable. Thread the webbing through the waist buckle(s), and pull the waist belt snug around the smallest part of your waist above your hips. (The webbing of an autolocking slide buckle is already threaded.) The waist belt must be tight enough that if you were to flip over, the harness would still be secure. Once the waist belt is tight, the belay loop should line up with your navel, and the middle of the back of the harness should line up with the middle of your back.

Legs. The leg loops should fit snugly around your upper thighs without interfering with movement. You should be able to comfortably slip two fingers between the leg loop and your thigh. If the waist belt fits properly but the leg loops do not, consider a harness with adjustable leg loops. Properly sized leg loops can still slide down your thigh, so tighten the rear keeper straps to minimize droopy leg loops.

Rise. Although waist-belt and leg-loop size is important, the distance of the waist belt from the leg loops should not be overlooked. This distance is referred to as the rise of the harness. Although there is no sizing for a harness's rise, test fitting is the best indication for proper length. More often, the harness's rise is too short rather than too long. A short rise creates a pull between the leg loops and the waist belt. This constant pull can be uncomfortable and may compromise the fit and function of the harness. In general, women need a longer rise and women-specific harnesses compensate for the gender difference. There are a few harness models with an adjustable rise, helping create the perfect fit.

Weighed fit. When you are standing on the ground, just about every properly fitting harness is comfortable. However, the true test of fit is hanging. Your climbing gear retailer should have a test rope. Make sure that you clip or tie in to both the leg-loop connector strap and the waist belt.

While hanging in the harness, pay attention to the distribution of pressure created by the waist belt and leg loops. It should be fairly even; this distribution of weight is a function of the harness's rise. A different rise may improve fit. Acute pressure on your lower back, sides of your waist, and legs depends on the padding, width, and shaping of the materials. Avoid any painful biting or pinching in these areas. Only after a weighted test should you make the decision to purchase a harness. The most expensive harness is not going to help you climb any better, so seek the best-fitting one.

Caring for Soft Gear

Harnesses and all other soft climbing gear are made of nylon. While light and strong, nylon is susceptible to chemical and ultraviolet light damage. Keep your nylon gear away from chemicals or other acidic substances, such as products containing acetic or citric acid, and even cat urine. If your gear comes in contact with questionable substances, retire the gear. When cleaning your gear to get rid of dirt or sweat, use a soft brush and a gentle soap or detergent without bleach. Rinse several times with cool, clean water and lay your gear to dry in a cool environment out of direct sunlight. Store your gear in a cool, dry place (again, not the trunk of your car in the summer) to prevent mold.

CARABINERS

Carabiners are links made of aluminum alloy or steel that a climber uses to connect pieces of gear, webbing, and ropes. A spring-loaded gate allows for the carabiner to be opened, and then the gate springs back into place to keep the carabiner closed. There are several carabiner body types, gates, and closures.

Nonlocking Gates

Nonlocking carabiners are used for attaching the rope or gear together. Clipping-end carabiners on lead climbs in the gym are nonlocking. They are easy to manipulate and open with ease. Easy opening has its drawbacks, though, especially when you want the gate closed. Multifunction straight-gate carabiners are the standard, while bent-gate carabiners make clipping the rope with one hand much easier. Wire gates reduce the overall weight of the carabiner, and their decreased mass over conventional gates makes them less likely to open from vibration.

Locking Gates

Locking carabiners provide more security at integral attachment points. An anchor carabiner or one used with a belay device should be secured with a locking mechanism. The most common locking mechanism is the screw lock, where a sleeve manually screws down to cover the carabiner gate and body and keep it from

Double-check locking carabiners before using them. While their locking mechanisms may be different (screw-lock gate, magnetic, etc.), they should be locked when in use.

opening. Common sense may tell you to screw down the locking sleeve until tight, but after a force weights the carabiner, the sleeve will further tighten, and then you may find yourself with a gate sleeve that will not unlock. Once the gate sleeve reaches its locking point, loosen the sleeve about a quarter turn. The gate will still be locked, but the sleeve will be loose enough to unscrew.

Autolocking and button-locking carabiners are alternatives to screw-lock gates. To open these gates, the user must first either rotate the locking sleeve or hold down a button while opening the carabiner. Personal preference and ease of opening are the deciding factors in which type of locking carabiner you use.

Shape

There are different carabiner body designs for many applications. Originally, all carabiners were symmetrically oval. From the oval design came the D-shaped carabiner, which puts more of the carabiner's load on the spine, increasing the carabiner's strength. Most carabiners used today are a modified offset D shape. The modification creates a wide end on one side and a narrow end on the other, maximizing the carabiner's strength-to-weight ratio. The smooth action of symmetrically shaped pear carabiners makes them a popular choice with tubular belay devices.

Strength

Carabiners are remarkably strong for their size and weight. However, the position of pull makes a difference in breaking strength. Carabiners are designed to be pulled along the axis of the spine with the gate closed; this orientation of pull offers the greatest strength of about 5,000 pounds of force. An open gate greatly compromises strength, holding only 1,500–2,000 pounds of force before failure. Cross-loading a carabiner by pulling across the spine and gate holds even less weight. Take care to ensure that the direction of pull on any carabiner is along the spine.

BELAY DEVICES

The belayer uses a belay device to help hold the climber in the event of a fall and to smoothly lower the climber in a controlled manner. The device attaches to the belayer's harness and to the climbing rope running through it, creating enough friction to allow the belayer to control the rope manually. For rock climbing, most belay devices can be used for rappelling or for descending a fixed rope, but these actions are not necessary in gym climbing. It is possible to belay without a belay device, but these techniques are less secure. Climbing gyms require the use of a device approved by the International Climbing and Mountaineering Federation (more commonly known as the UIAA, or the Union Internationale des Associations d'Alpinisme).

Tubular Belay Devices

Tubular belay devices are popular among climbers. A loop of rope is pushed into the device and clipped with a locking carabiner. Rope feeds through the belay device, and in the event of a fall, the series of bends in the rope through the device can create enough friction to lock the rope in place. The belayer simply holds the rope in the appropriate orientation to allow for maximum friction. Tubular belay devices are popular

A tubular belay device locks the rope when the brake hand holds the rope securely below the device, creating enough friction to prevent the rope from slipping.

for their versatility as a rappel device, their low cost, and their light weight.

There are many variations of the tubular device, all working on the same principles. Gaining popularity are grooved devices with teeth, where the brake strand runs over the side of the device. These grooves increase the amount of surface area between the rope and device, thus creating more friction and increasing holding power.

Assisted-Braking Belay Devices

Assisted-braking devices provide more friction than traditional tubular belay devices. This additional braking power makes it easier for the belayer to catch a climber, requiring less human holding power. Not all assisted-braking belay devices are designed, or even operate, the same. It's

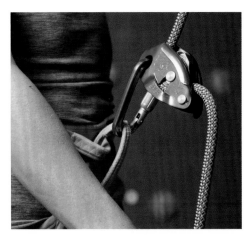

An assisted-braking belay device, like the GriGri depicted here, maintains friction while the rope is weighted, which can make the belay system more secure than a traditional tubular device.

very important to refer to the manufacturer's instructions.

The Petzl GriGri is the most popular assisted-braking belay device. Larger, heavier, and more costly than a tubular device, GriGris have an assist mechanism that can slowly feed out rope, but quick movement (like a falling climber) clamps the locking device down on the rope, pinching it in place. A lever releases the pinch and controls the climber's descent. GriGris are very popular with gym and sport climbers. Because of the popularity of this device, you'll see it as the prominent belay device depicted in this book.

Caring for Hardware

Metal climbing hardware (like carabiners and belay devices) is susceptible to invisible hairline fractures if dropped onto hard surfaces. Since padding covers most gym climbing floors, such damage is not a problem indoors. Still, develop a healthy respect for your gear.

Over time, the moving parts of your hardware (like the gate hinges or locking sleeves of carabiners) can become caked with dirt, which affects the piece's mechanics. Give your gear some tender loving care by applying a lubricant, such as WD-40, will loosen the grime and keep the parts moving freely. Also identify it with tape or some other marking that does not structurally affect the metal. It is easy to mix up equipment with other climbers in the gym since gear choices are limited.

ROPE

Serving as the lifeline between the climber and belayer, a rope is engineered to meet climbing's impact demands. You won't need your own rope right away; you will need one only once you start lead climbing, if your gym doesn't already provide them. While it is important to understand how a climbing rope works to improve your safety, the decision of what model or diameter rope to use while top-roping in the gym is already made for you. This way, gym employees can inspect and replace the ropes at regular intervals and manage the number of people climbing routes at a given time. You'll need to bring your own rope to the gym only if they don't provide them for you for lead climbing.

The dynamic properties of climbing ropes allow them to elongate with the force

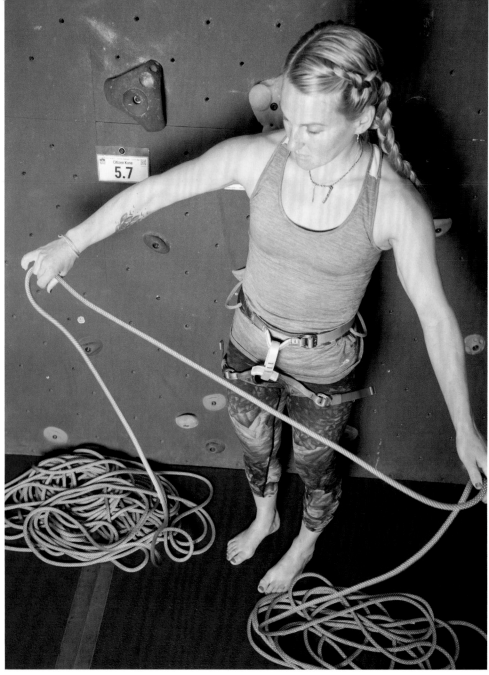

Whether it's the gym's or your own, take care of the rope by keeping it free of kinks, and avoid stepping on it.

of a fall. Imagine how uncomfortable (and dangerous) it would feel to take even a short fall with a steel cable attached to your waist. Although less elastic than a bungee cord, a climbing rope's elasticity increases the time it takes for the climber to stop. The longer it takes to slow the fall, the less force the fall generates on the climber and the rest of the anchor system. The amount of stretch is also proportional to the amount of rope that is stretching between the climber and belayer. For example, falling at the bottom of a forty-foot top rope (when approximately eighty feet of rope travels from the belayer to the top anchors and back down to the climber) creates more rope stretch than falling at the top of the same climb (from the top, only slightly more than forty feet of rope connects the climber to the belayer). Keep this in mind when starting a top-rope climb. New ropes elongate much farther than used ones, and smaller-diameter ropes stretch more than thicker ropes.

A climbing rope is constructed with an inner core and an outer sheath. The dynamic properties of the rope are in the core, which is composed of nylon filaments twisted together that stretch under the force of a fall and then slowly contract. The outer sheath is merely the protective casing for the core. Together, the core and sheath create a diameter of between nine and eleven millimeters for a single climbing rope. With the high climbing traffic in gyms, expect to use a ten- to eleven-millimeter-diameter rope with a durable sheath. Although not needed in the gym, you can buy a rope with

a dry treatment for inclement weather. The sheath, core, or sometimes both receive a chemical treatment that prevents the rope from absorbing water.

Treat any rope you use with care, and trust your life to it. Stepping on the rope pushes dirt and dust into it, potentially compromising its longevity. When walking with a rope, pick it up, rather than dragging it across the floor. Always inspect your rope after every climbing session—run your hands over the length of the rope, looking for abnormal signs of sheath wear.

GEAR CONSIDERATIONS

Other gear you may want includes chalk, belay gloves, a helmet, and activity-specific clothing.

CHALK

Just as gymnasts use chalk to dry their hands and improve their grip, climbers do the same. The simplest form of chalk is carbonate magnesium, which comes in blocks to be crushed by the user. Powdered blends of chalk specifically designed for climbing are offered by several companies. These compounds have drying agents that can cause excessive hand dryness for some users. Because loose chalk can create a white haze and less-than-desirable air quality without sufficient ventilation, some gyms do not allow it. The alternative is a chalk ball, which is a thin "sock" packed with chalk. Grabbing the ball slightly powders the hand, and most chalk balls are refillable. Chalk is predominately white in

Wear your chalk bag in the center of your back so that it is easier to dip into it with either hand.

makes it easier to get your hands covered. Of course, make sure your hand fits into the bag. Chalk bags have cinch straps to keep them closed when not in use. A chalk bag that closes securely will keep your climbing pack from sporting a constant dusting of chalk. Since chalk bags come in so many different patterns, colors, and fabrics (you can even have them custom made, or if you're crafty, make one for yourself), they are one of the few climbing accessories you can match to your personality!

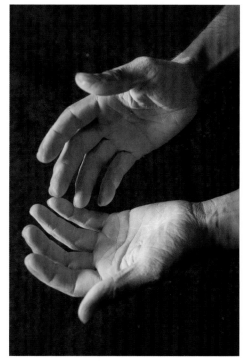

Liquid chalk applies like a lotion and dries within a few minutes. It's a great alternative if your gym prohibits loose chalk.

color, but there are some environmentally friendly colors like brown and tan for outdoor use. Applying liquid chalk can also help sweaty hands. Liquid chalk is a fine chalk-and-alcohol blend that is applied directly to the hands and dries quickly, leaving the hands with a dry chalky coating.

Bags to hold the chalk are hung in the middle of the back, attached directly to the harness or its own belt or strap. There are some minor differences in the function of a chalk bag. Look for one that is fully lined with fleece. This lining absorbs chalk and

BELAY GLOVES

If your hands are sensitive to holding the rope while belaying and lowering a climber, consider specially designed belay gloves. These gloves have a snug fit and a thin leather palm to provide protection from the rope running through the belayer's hands. This can build confidence in the belayer's ability to hold and lower a climber. Gloves also keep the belayer's hands clean from residue that comes off the rope. Before using belay gloves, consider using a different belay device that may provide more holding power, because gloves decrease the belayer's sensitivity to the rope.

HELMET

While climbing outdoors, wearing a helmet is a safe practice. Helmets protect climbers from rocks and other falling objects. In the gym, however, helmets are seldom worn since falling objects are less likely than in outdoor rock climbing (carabiners can still fall, though). New climbers and young children should wear helmets to protect their heads in case they lose their balance and bump into the wall. Traditional climbing-specific helmets are constructed with a hard plastic designed to take repeated abuse. Newer helmets with softer shells are lighter and more breathable but are less durable and require greater care.

CLOTHING

Like any other activity or sport, climbing has its own activity-specific clothing. The leopard print climbing tights of the late 1980s are extinct, and designers have moved

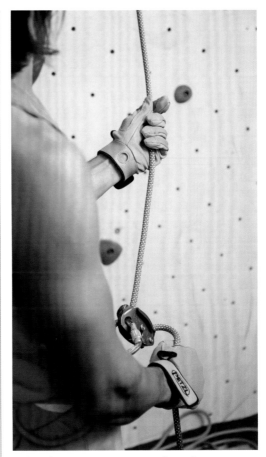

Belay gloves can secure your grip and protect your hands. Before using them, learn how to belay without gloves to develop a better "feel" for belaying and lowering.

to a more functional blend with popular fashion. Current fabrics are durable yet soft, and stretchy materials allow for unhindered movement and a maximum range of motion. Wicking fabrics help keep climbers cool, too. Shirts and pullovers are cut trim at the waist to easily fit under a harness, and fitted sleeves stay out of the way of grabbing holds. Pants or long shorts can protect the knees from scrapes and bruises, while tapered legs improve visibility of the feet for precise footwork. A bulky waistband on pants can be uncomfortable with a harness, so climb in something with a low-profile waist. Specific garments are not a necessity, though, and any clothes that serve the mentioned functions are fine. Yoga-specific apparel works quite well, for example. Durability isn't as much an issue in gym climbing as it is in rock climbing outdoors.

PURCHASING EQUIPMENT

You trust your life to the gear you purchase and use. With this in mind, make sure that everything fits and functions properly. Try on all your equipment, and get an expert opinion on its fit. Try to fit your gear at the same place you will purchase it. Due to the importance of safety for climbing gear, most retailers do not take returns on safety equipment (carabiners, harnesses, etc.) even if the product is unused. This further emphasizes the importance of proper fit before making purchases.

ONLINE

Online stores have gained popularity with their discount prices and ease of purchasing, but unfortunately, you cannot try the gear on, and in-person customer service is not available. Purchasing an item that you have already owned or tried on would be appropriate, though. You can find excellent closeout or overstock deals on climbing gear through websites and mail order. However, if a retail store provides you with customer service, they deserve your patronage.

OUTDOOR STORES

General sporting-goods stores that have climbing departments tend to offer the smallest selection of gear and the least-experienced staff. Outdoor stores are a better bet for well-stocked climbing departments and knowledgeable staff. Since employees may be assigned to different departments, ask for a climbing specialist. Do not work with someone who knows less than you do.

CLIMBING-SPECIFIC SHOPS

Climbing-specific retailers are an excellent source of climbing gear. Usually located near outdoor climbing destinations, these shops hire climbers who have practical experience with the gear they sell. Most likely, a small climbing wall will be available to fit test gear before purchasing. The selection is usually up to date with the latest gear innovations.

CLIMBING GYMS

A majority of climbing gyms have some sort of retail shop, although the selection of gear varies widely. Often, larger gyms have a greater retail selection. As a gym climber, you'll benefit from seeking information about, getting fitted, and purchasing gear from the same people that you see in the gym on a regular basis.

Support your local climbing gym's retail shop. They're often the most qualified experts in the gear and equipment you need.

Climbing gyms are often the site of gear demonstrations, or "demos." Climbing gear representatives (often from shoe and harness companies) bring in products for climbers to try out on the wall. This is the most effective way to try out gear and decide what you like. With a manufacturer's representative present, you can find the perfect fit and get answers to any technical questions. Ask your gym about the frequency of gear demos.

USED GEAR

For the key pieces of safety equipment, used gear is not recommended. It is important to know firsthand the history of nylon items and hardware. Nylon items (like a harness) that have been exposed to harmful solvents (like battery acid or bleach) should not be used, even if they pass a visual inspection. Carabiners and belay devices may look new, but having been dropped from even a nominal height can affect their integrity.

Purchasing used climbing shoes is less of a safety issue—although they may present hygienic concerns—so make your own decisions on their value and condition. Online auction sites sell plenty of used gear, and most climbing gyms have bulletin boards with postings for used gear. Purchasing used shoes for children whose feet are still growing is an economical move for parents.

GEAR STANDARDS AND TESTING

The International Climbing and Mountaineering Federation (Union Internationale des Associations d'Alpinisme, or UIAA) is a governing body that sets safety standards of climbing gear. Their laboratory tests set minimum standards for safety equipment such as ropes, sewn nylon products (like webbing and harnesses), carabiners, and belay devices. Climbing gear companies conduct their own tests for product development and safety measures, usually (but not always) to meet UIAA guidelines. In general, gym climbing gear available for purchase at established climbing retailers meets or exceeds UIAA standards. Do not take your own safety for granted, though. For more information on the technical specifications of particular equipment, contact the manufacturer.

Opposite: *Climbing movement is a balance of power and grace.*

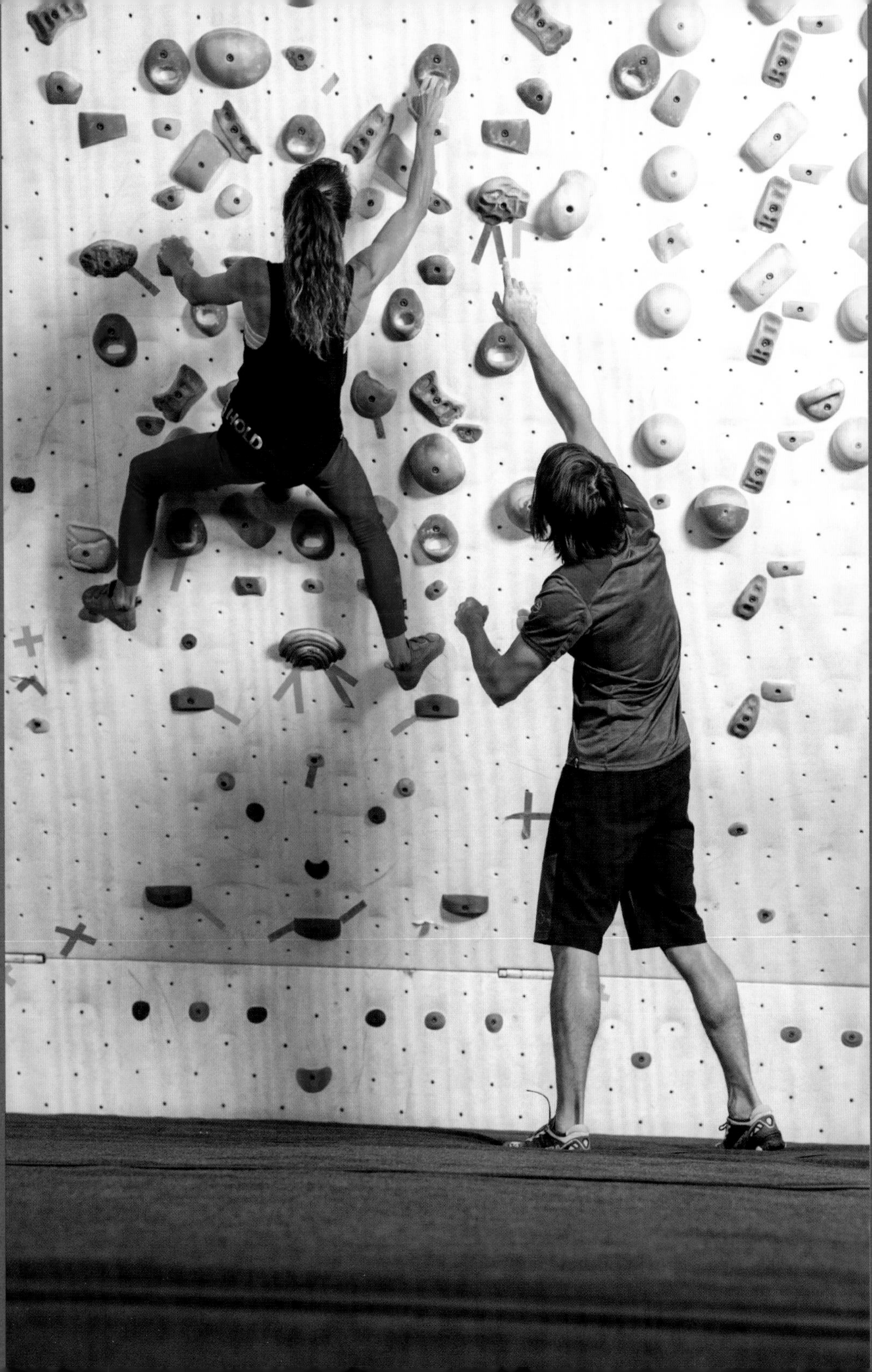
HOLD

CHAPTER 3

Movement Technique

Power and grace—the two characteristics that best describe an experienced climber. Climbing movement is just the climber moving in accordance to the holds available. An experienced climber's moves look effortless, while a new climber executing what is essentially a series of pull-ups can appear jerky and awkward.

For most new climbers, the main objective is to get to the top of the wall or route. While the satisfaction of this accomplishment alone may provide an incentive to keep climbing, most people strive to challenge themselves by trying more difficult climbs as their ability improves. One way to climb more difficult routes is to become physically stronger, but these improvements are limiting. Climbing is often thought to rely primarily on the strength of the upper body, as if the number of pull-ups you can do is an indicator of how hard you can climb. After just a few climbs, though, it becomes evident that technique and movement skills play a more important role in climbing movement than raw strength. The fastest and most efficient way to become a better climber is by improving your technique.

This chapter focuses on learning the proper climbing technique on all types of terrain and angles. From less-than-vertical terrain to steep routes on an overhang, climbing techniques differ. It is important to have a solid foundation of the skills discussed in this chapter to be a proficient all-around climber.

TYPES OF MOVEMENT

Climbers characterized as smooth and graceful often display static movement as opposed to dynamic movement. Static moves are initiated and maintained via musculature. For example, standing on the tips of your toes to reach a hold rather than jumping to it is a static move.

The primary advantage of static movement is control. Static climbing requires balance throughout the move. This balance allows you to let go of a handhold or foothold and reach or step to the desired position. If your body is stable as you reach, you have the opportunity to search for the best part of the handhold, or be ready to shift your weight back onto your foot. If you can pause in the middle of the move, you are climbing with static technique.

Static movement is what every beginning climber should strive for because it forces proper body positioning and balance. However, static movement has its limitations. If you simply cannot reach the hold from a static position, dynamic movement is a more appropriate technique for extending your reach.

In dynamic, or momentum-based, movement, the body is set in motion in an attempt to "carry" itself to a hold. The most extreme form of dynamic movement would be flight, when a climber jumps up to latch on to a hold. More subtle forms of dynamic movement would be small jabs to holds that the climber cannot reach in a static position. A disadvantage to dynamic movement is that once the body is set in motion, there are no last-second opportunities to correct body positioning. In addition, you have only one chance to grab the best part of the hold you are shooting for and stick to it. (See Dynamic Movement toward the end of this chapter.)

PERFECT PRACTICE

The saying "practice makes perfect" is true only to a point, since whatever you practice is what you perfect, and practicing bad habits is not helpful in the long run. Consider instead that "perfect practice makes perfect." It is just as easy to ingrain bad habits as it is to learn good habits. If you just climb, without regard for technique,

you might get better, but inefficient habits will become so learned that your progress will be limited. Deliberately practicing the foundations of climbing movement will help you learn faster and progress with ease in the future.

CHARACTERISTICS OF A GOOD CLIMBER

The next time you are in the gym, look around at the people climbing. Try to identify someone who you think is a graceful climber, regardless of how hard or easy their climb is. Perhaps you have already noticed such climbers. Consider what characteristics make that person a good climber.

Good climbers have the ability to shift from one move to another without interrupting their movement. This kind of fluid movement is referred to simply as "flow," and without it, a climber's moves can look jerky, disconnected, and maybe even desperate. To achieve a flow of movement, the climber looks as though he already knows what every move is supposed to be like and which holds to use and when. Each move is deliberate, with little wasted movement, making the task look effortless as the climber seemingly floats up the wall. A popular analogy is that great climbers look as though they are dancing up the wall. Just as a dancer's movement is dictated by the rhythm and sound of the music, a climber's body positioning is dictated by the holds and features on the wall.

In line with this analogy, a climber, like a dancer, must master many steps before tackling more complex moves. For example, before you can dance, you must learn some basic steps and footwork. Before that, a strong command of walking is necessary. And on the most basic level, you must be able to stand and have basic balance skills. Climbing movement must be approached the same way. A sound sense of balance, proper weight shifting, and foot precision are key components that lead to total body movement.

WEIGHT SHIFTING

The general principle for all types of climbing is to get as much of your body weight on your legs as possible, and use your legs to push off for upward movement and your upper body to help maintain balance and posture. Thus, your ability to shift your weight over your feet is a fundamental skill. This is true for all types of climbing terrain, although there are some modifications in body positioning on steep, overhanging climbs.

Your ability to control your center of gravity relies on weight shifting. Generally, a woman's center of gravity is in the area of the hips, and a man's center of gravity tends to be a bit higher. If you were to stand with your feet shoulder-width apart with weight evenly distributed on both feet, your center of gravity would pull down directly between your feet, splitting your body in two.

Looking back at the dancing analogy, you must learn to walk before you can dance. From standing with your feet shoulder-width apart, consider what your center of gravity must do to allow you to step forward. To step with your left foot, your center of gravity must shift over the right foot to free up the left. The same weight shifting occurs in climbing, though the difference is in stepping up, not forward.

The width of your stance plays a significant role in weight shifting. When your feet are close together, your center of gravity needs to move only mere inches to shift your weight, whereas wide stances require your center of gravity to move much farther. Another benefit of a close stance is maximum reach, but consider that standing with your feet close together is not very stable. For getting started, standing with your feet shoulder-width apart is the best of both worlds.

BALANCE CHECKLIST FOR VERTICAL TERRAIN
- Keep as much weight on the inside edges of your feet as possible with your heels up for maximum reach.
- Maintain an upright posture to limit slouching.
- Pull your hips toward the wall, as if a string were pulling your belly button over your feet.
- Relax your upper body.

When you shift your center of gravity, it is important that the movement comes from your hips, not your upper body or shoulders. Leaning is not sufficient for complete weight shifting. Proper weight shifting comes from deep bends in the legs, allowing the hips to move back and forth. Horizontal weight shifting should occur before moving up.

Pay attention to how close your center of gravity is from the wall. On vertical terrain, the closer you are to the wall, the more weight your legs sustain, and your arms will be less taxed. Your center of gravity will move slightly away from the wall while you are stepping with your feet, so it is essential to pull your hips close into the wall between moves. Visualize a string attached to your belly button, pulling you tight into the wall. Your shoulders should be arched back a bit, allowing you to look up and around at your environment. Avoid hugging the wall with your upper body, for this creates the tendency for your hips to sag away from the wall.

Although we can draw parallels between walking and stepping up while climbing, the use of hands in rock climbing tends to complicate weight shifting. When walking on the ground, you have no other choice than to effectively shift your weight to step forward. But since climbing is thought to be an upper-body-intensive activity, climbers tend to overuse their arms simply because they can. What often happens is that a climber grips holds with her hands, supporting her weight by her arms instead

Edge precision can be the difference between standing with confidence and slipping unexpectedly.

of properly shifting her weight from one foot to the other. This happens even with advanced climbers who use underdeveloped footwork and weight shifting. Overuse of your upper body will cause you to tire quickly. Because you can stand on your feet all day long but hang from your arms for only a few minutes, minimize pulling with your arms as much as possible.

KEY EXERCISE: LEARNING PROPER WEIGHT SHIFTING

Smooth and efficient movement comes from properly shifting your center of gravity over your feet. By learning how to move by pushing with the legs and using only the hands for balance, you are less likely to overuse your upper body and will tire less quickly.

The Goal: Balanced, controlled, smooth movement on less-than-vertical terrain initiated from the legs.

The Setup: Position the footholds near the ground creating a horizontal traverse. The holds should be relatively close together and the height of each should vary by no more than one foot.

NO-HANDS TRAVERSE EXERCISE

1. Using the palms of your hands against the wall for balance, step onto the leftmost foothold from the ground with your right foot.
2. Once balanced on your right foot, bring your left foot next to it on the hold.
3. Shift your weight from your right foot onto your left foot. This should free up the right foot so you can move it.

Matt keeps his center of gravity over his feet with a relaxed upper body, showing that he has a strong foundation of balance.

4. Step to the next hold with the right foot. Shift your hips over your right foot to take weight off the left foot.

5. Repeat these steps until the end of the traverse has been reached, and then come back in the other direction.

CONSIDERATIONS

- Lightly use handholds for balance if necessary.
- Remember to fully weight and unweight your feet before moving. Laterally shift, and then stand.
- Move slowly enough that you could stop your movement at any time. Avoid falling onto holds, and practice stepping down as much as stepping up.
- Pay attention to the guidelines in the Balance Checklist for Vertical Terrain (page 54).

Since this is done near the ground, it's a great exercise if you do not have any belaying or top-roping experience. The angle steepness of the wall, size of the footholds, and the spacing of the holds all contribute to the difficulty of this exercise. Changing any one of these can make the exercise more or less difficult to suit your current level of balance and movement. Once you feel comfortable performing the exercise, increase the challenge.

By keeping her hips close to the wall and weight balanced between her feet, this climber doesn't even need to use handholds!

FOOT PRECISION IN WEIGHT SHIFTING

Edging, using the inside edge of your foot when standing on holds, is the most common type of foot placement. This technique allows you to rotate your foot around the hold for better balance, keeps you in line with your center of gravity when shifting your weight, and allows you to stand on your toes to gain maximum height. When using the inside edge of your foot, it is important to create contact between the hold and the outside edge of your toe. This allows your foot to rotate on that single point to adjust body positioning. In this balanced and frontal position, your toes will be pointed out in a duck-toed fashion. This is helpful when stepping because it allows the hips to stay close to the wall. If you stepped up with your feet pointed straight into the wall, your hips would be pushed out, creating more weight for your arms to bear.

Use as much of the toe of the shoe and inside of the pocket as possible.

FOOTWORK

As previously mentioned, edging is a popular form of foot positioning. However, there will be many instances where there is no edging platform on which to stand. Consider the following alternatives.

POCKETS

There are usually two options for using pocket-like holds as footholds in an indoor environment. If the pocket is big enough or your shoes are amply pointed, place as much of your toe box in the hold as possible, and use the front edge of the toe box (the pointiest part). If that does not provide

When smearing, create as much surface area as possible between the shoe rubber and climbing surface by lowering your heel and pushing into the wall, not down.

enough security, try standing on top of the entire hold. Your ability to use pockets as footholds is somewhat dependent on your footwear. Rental and beginner's shoes usually have a very rounded toe that is less than desirable on small to moderate pockets.

SMEARING

Sloping edges, or "slopers," those that slope away from the wall and down toward the ground, are more difficult to stand on since the foot has a tendency to slide off the hold. The more surface area between the hold and your shoe, the better the friction. Smearing is the most exaggerated form of standing on a sloping hold, used when there simply are no footholds to step on. This technique relies solely on creating enough tension and surface area between the sole of the foot and the wall. Dropping the heel below the toes and leaning the body away from the wall pushes the climber's center of gravity in toward the wall instead of down to the ground. This method does create a lot of stress on the arms because of the limited amount of weight that smearing can hold before the foot slips.

HEEL AND TOE HOOKS

Rather than stepping on a hold with the edge of your foot, hooking the hold with your foot can sometimes be a more effective way for your feet to support your body. Heel hooks are often used on overhanging faces, when pulling over roofs—steep to horizontal "ceilings" overhead—or around corners (also known as arêtes), for example. The advantage of placing your heel on or

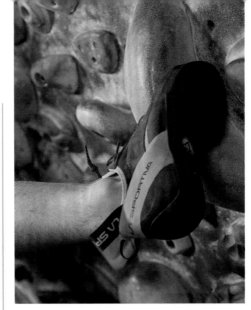

For a toe hook, keep the toes flexed and use your toes or top of your foot as a "hook."

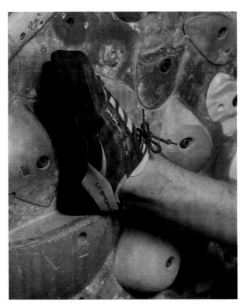

A heel hook requires a climber to maintain consistent pressure on a hold with his heel. Constant pressure will keep the heel engaged on the hold.

around a foothold is that it provides a solid platform from which to pull your hips closer to the hold. In this instance, it would be more difficult, if not impossible, to get your toes around the hold and pull in. Do not be afraid to pull in tight with your hamstrings to get your hips locked in close to the wall. The higher you can position your hips, the closer the next handholds will be.

Toe hooks are used in similar instances to heel hooks, but the toes are flexed up toward the knee and locked into that position. From this locked position, your foot can be used as a hook, latching on to underclings, corners, and the backsides of holds. To stay locked into position and to keep your hips from sagging, pull your foot toward your hips to maintain body tension throughout the move. Solid heel and toe hooks are a sneaky way to find rests on every type of terrain.

TOE AND FOOT JAMS

Jamming your hands or feet into cracks is usually reserved for outdoor rock climbing, but these techniques should not be over-looked by the indoor climber. Some gyms have beautifully sculpted crack systems that include holds designed as cracks. You can even use crack techniques on two holds placed close together or in a corner.

If you are stepping into a crack with your right foot, roll your ankle to the out-side so that the sole of your foot is facing to the left. In this position, your toes are perpendicular to the ground and your knee points out to the right. Slide your toes into the crack as far as they will go. To secure

the jam, rotate your knee so it points straight up. This will provide the torque needed to keep your foot secure, and now it can be weighted. If you relax the pressure created on your foot in the crack at any point during the movement, your foot will likely slide out.

FLAGGING

Climbers do not always have the luxury of two solid footholds to stand on or move from. Often, there is only one foothold that allows for efficient body positioning. In these instances, adjust your center of gravity using your upper body for positioning so that as much of your weight as possible is on that one foothold. You may need to rotate your body to use the outside edge of your foot. The foot without a hold can then "flag" against the wall with its inside edge, helping to stabilize the body. This flagging foot acts like a rudder by pushing against the wall, keeping the hips close to the wall and over the weighted foot. If the holdless foot is not placed against the wall and left to dangle, it can create a barn-door effect. That is, the holdless foot swings away from the wall and pulls the rest of the body with it.

Flagging with the outside edge of the foot can be helpful, too. In this position, the weighted foot uses its inside edge. The flagging foot can either be crossed through your body between the weighted leg and the wall, or it can be positioned behind the weighted leg, pinning it against the wall. Most often, outside-edge flagging is more effective when the latter technique is employed.

Above: *With his right foot flagged in front of his left leg, to the left of his body, Matt can stand on his left foot. This technique is beneficial when holds are sparse, unlike on the wall shown here.*
Below: *With his right foot flagged behind his left leg and to the left of his body, Matt's right hip is locked into place, helping him stabilize his body so that he can reach upward.*

KEY EXERCISE: LEARNING FOOT PLACEMENT AND PRECISION

When advanced climbers perform their art, their movement speaks for itself. With less advanced climbers, the thud of a misplaced foot against the wall says a lot, too. Noise from a climber's foot scraping or sliding down the wall to reach a foothold results from sloppy foot placements. This comes from either imbalanced movement or not paying enough attention to the desired target.

In ball sports like soccer, baseball, or golf, if the participant takes his eyes off the ball too early by looking in the anticipated direction of travel, contact with the ball is less likely. The same holds true for climbing. A common mistake is looking down to find a foothold only long enough for the foot to get near or above the hold. At the last second, there is a tendency to look up for the next move. This premature search for holds produces a margin of error in foot placement.

The Goal: Learn to prevent the common "touch and slide" placement, that is, putting the foot against the wall and grinding it down until it lands on the hold. This grinding makes the climber unable to put the foot in the maximum weighted position on the hold because the foot interferes with the climber's line of vision. The excessive grinding also quickly destroys the climbing shoe's rubber. "Quiet" feet force the climber to move more slowly as well, due to the desire for efficient placement.

The Setup: Pick a route that you are interested in climbing. It can also be a traverse. Your belayer or spotter (if on a traverse near the ground) can help you by pointing out your loud footwork.

QUIET FEET AND STARE-DOWN EXERCISE

1. Climb a route and concentrate on keeping your feet as quiet as possible.
2. For every hold that you step on, make sure that you focus on the hold and "stare it down" until your foot is firmly placed on the hold.
3. Your belayer or climbing partner (if you are traversing near the ground) should announce every time she hears your footwork.

Not only is this an exercise, but it is also what you should strive for in your climbing on a regular basis. Precise footwork will give you confidence, and you will not have to second-guess your foot placements.

STEMMING

Stemming is an effective way to rest inside of corners, or "dihedrals." By pushing with your feet against the walls of the corner, a substantial amount of weight can be taken off your arms. Your hands can also stem by pushing away from each other. This can free up a foot to step up and make vertical progress.

HIGH-STEPS

When stepping up on footholds positioned near the waist, flexibility can be a limiting factor for some people. Even if you can get your foot on the hold, using it to your full advantage can be difficult. For high foot placements, focus on pointing your knee out to the side of your body when stepping up. If you step up with your knee pointed into the wall, your hips will be pushed back from the wall, causing you to fall away from the wall. Once your foot is on the hold, shifting all your weight onto your foot can be difficult, since you are per-forming a one-legged squat to push your body up the wall.

BODY POSITIONING

The location of a handhold dictates how you grab the hold and what body posi-tioning is required to allow you to hold on to it with as little effort as possible. Since your arm can fully rotate in front of you, there are endless possibilities for where a hold may be in relation to your body. Con-sider the following four positions and the body positions they require.

When resting, or hanging, on one arm, keep it as straight as possible to let your bones take the weight and your muscles relax.

STRAIGHT ON

This is the most basic and natural hand position. Reaching up and grabbing the top of a hold is a straight-on position. The palm faces away from the climber, toward the

KEY EXERCISE: LEARNING TO CLIMB WITH THE LEGS

The importance of efficient footwork and body positioning cannot be emphasized enough. Climbers tend to pull down with their hands, even when they do not need to.

The Goal: Learn to generate upward movement by pushing with the legs more than by pulling with the arms. This exercise is very similar to the No-Hands Traverse Exercise but is geared toward vertical rather than horizontal movement.

The Setup: Tie in to the rope as the climber. The climb should be very easy with a lot of footholds and handholds. Do not worry about staying on an established route.

LOW-HANDS CLIMBING EXERCISE

1. Climb a route keeping your hands as low as possible. Shoot for not reaching above your head.
2. Since climbing with low hands limits your ability to pull down on holds, reach out to the sides and use handholds to help shift your weight from side to side, and gain vertical ground by pushing with your legs.

CONSIDERATIONS

- Start this exercise on a less-than-vertical wall and then work up to more challenging terrain. Remember, the idea behind these exercises is not just to get to the top of the climb, but to learn and practice skills through the exercise itself.
- As you feel more comfortable with this exercise, try to position your hands lower.
- Since your hands are used only for lateral pulling in this exercise, they should not be tired at the end of the climb.
- Climbing with low hands is not recommended as a regular climbing style, but as an exercise, it is effective in forcing deep weight shifting.

wall, and the fingertips extend above the wrist. Keep your arm as straight as possible. This allows the bone structure in your arms to take your body weight. A bent arm flexes the muscles and can speed up fatigue.

UNDERCLING

The opposite of grabbing a hold straight on is an undercling. With this type of grip, the hand rotates inward so the palm is facing away from the wall. The closer the hold is to the body, the easier it is to maintain control. Grabbing an undercling at full arm extension requires significant body tension, so the closer the hold is "pulled down" to the hips, the more stable the body becomes, because the biceps are used to pull the hips in. The sooner you can get your feet

To use a sidepull (right hand shown here), climbers often must adjust their body position significantly to help them pull sideways instead of down.

Because of the awkward elbow positioning required to hold on to a gaston (left hand shown here), be careful not to put too much pressure on the shoulder that is pulling down on the hold.

up and bring the hold closer to your body, the better. Although they can be found on all types of terrain, look for underclings in roofs.

SIDEPULL

Reaching out on a face to grab a corner is a classic example of using a sidepull. With this grip, there is no way to pull down on the hold, so you must shift your weight to lean away from the "positive" side of the hold—the side that provides greater purchase—creating enough tension for stability or movement.

GASTON

The gaston is a sort of "pushing" sidepull. If the positive part of a sidepull is facing you, use a backhanded grip to reach for the hold with your palm facing outward. To create tension on the hold, shift your weight toward it as much as possible. Keep your elbow pointing away from your body if possible, and maintain pressure with your foot on the side opposite the handhold. This position can create a lot of stress on the shoulders, so practice it with care.

HAND GRIPS

In addition to using your hands in body positioning, various holds require different grips.

EDGES

Ranging from pencil-thin to large enough to sit on, edges make up a significant portion of the grips used in climbing. The size and angle of the edge determine how to grab the

A closed-hand crimp, with the knuckles angled up and thumb wrapped around the index finger, puts an incredible amount of stress on the tendons in the fingers. Be sure to warm up to full crimping strength.

hold. The easiest types of edges are incut, meaning they slope downward toward the wall, allowing the fingers to slide to the back of the hold and stay relatively secure there. Sloping edges are difficult to grab since there is no positive grip on the hold, and the fingers fight just to stay in contact with the hold. Consider the following types of grips on edges.

Using the same hold depicted in the closed-hand crimp, an open-hand grip puts less stress on the finger tendons but requires more forearm strength to keep the fingers stable.

For two-finger pockets, pairing the middle and ring finger is the strongest combination. For three-finger pockets, add the pointer finger.

Crimping

Crimping is holding on to an edge with the second knuckle pointing up. The thumb can be added for additional force and stability. This grip is very strenuous because your body weight is supported by the joints of your fingers. The pads of your fingertips are in contact with the hold's surface and are bent back at the first joint. Because crimping requires less hand strength than an open-hand grip, beginning climbers tend to use this grip more often. Finger injuries usually involve crimping.

Open Hand

An alternative to crimping is the open grip. This position is friendlier to tendons since the knuckles are buckled less severely, but it requires more forearm strength because the tendons and forearm muscles, rather

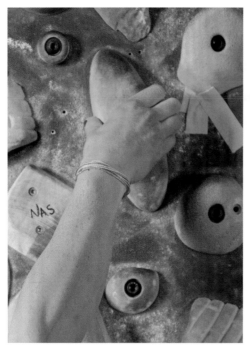

Narrow pinches can feel awkward, but focus on generating force with all four fingers and the thumb.

For wide pinches, try to get as many fingers engaged in the squeeze as possible.

than the joints, absorb body weight. Try to grab edges in an open grip as much as possible to help prevent finger injuries. You may find it difficult at first, but the strength will come quickly.

POCKETS

Pockets can range from handlebar-like jugs—deep incut holds that allow you to grip them like a handlebar—to sloping one-finger nightmares. Gripping a pocket with your fingers is a bit like stuffing your feet into climbing shoes. Stacking your fingers in a pocket creates pressure that increases the friction and provides a more secure hold. The more fingers you can get into the hold and the deeper you can sink them, the better.

PINCHES

Grabbing a hold with an open grip and using the thumb to squeeze the hold is known as pinching. Any hold, from as wide as a telephone pole to as thin as a cigar, can be pinched, but the difficulty lies in creating enough force in the hands and forearms to grasp the hold. The wider the grip, the more difficult it is to create force on the hold.

KEY EXERCISE: LEARNING TO CLIMB BY FEEL

Of all our senses, sight often takes over as the primary receptor, and decisions we make while climbing are mainly sight dependent. But much of the visual stimuli we take in is irrelevant to climbing, and we can become overwhelmed with information. When climbers make judgments based on sight, they may shy away from holds that look sloping or too small to use. Also, the more that climbers depend on sight, the less they rely on spatial awareness. Understanding how your body relates to an environment is invaluable, saving time wasted on visually searching for footholds that you have already used as handholds.

Climbing blindfolded can help overcome this challenge. Not only does it help you develop spatial awareness and feel, but it also forces your body to climb statically and to stay in balance. When you search with your hand to find a hold, the rest of your body must be in balance to compensate for the time that the free hand is searching. This is true for the feet as well. Note that dynamic movement is effective only when seeking predetermined targets and ineffective while climbing blind.

The Goal: Learn to develop spatial awareness, the sensation of climbing by feel, and climbing "in the moment" without visual distraction.

The Setup: Make sure that there are enough holds on the climb. Remember, you will be blindfolded, so staying on route is impossible. Tie in to the rope, and perform a safety check with your belayer before putting on the blindfold. Make sure your belayer lets you know when you are near the top.

BLINDFOLDED CLIMBING EXERCISE

1. Take your time stepping onto the route. To stay in balance and find holds, you will be climbing much slower than you would normally.
2. When searching for holds, make large sweeping motions and search in all directions.
3. The belayer should be silent during this exercise. Giving verbal guidance will only distract the climber from the task at hand. The belayer should announce to the climber when he is near the top.
4. Take off the blindfold before being lowered to the ground.

CONSIDERATIONS

- This exercise is most effective on easy, less-than-vertical terrain.
- Increase the challenge by limiting the number of holds, rather than increasing the steepness of the terrain.

This is a great exercise for new climbers who are anxious about climbing or height. It enables them to focus solely on climbing and not on the discomfort of being off the ground. They must be prepared to take their blindfold off at the top of the climb, though.

SLOPERS

Sloping holds are the trickiest set of holds to master. Since they slope down away from the wall, the surface area is such that your hands feel like they are slipping and sliding right off the hold. Because there is no incut area to dig your fingers into, you'll rely on contact with the surface area and your direction of pull to hang on to the sloper. The more surface area of your hand that is in contact with the hold, the more friction created and the better you will grasp the hold. On large slopers, consider contacting the hold not with just your hands, but your wrists and forearms, too. Also, keeping your center of gravity low and beneath the hold will prevent you from sliding off it.

When pulling the hold down and raising your body to move past the sloper, maintain that downward force by keeping your elbow directly under the sloper. Raising the elbow will change the direction of pull from down to out, causing your hand to slip off the hold.

HAND JAMS AND FINGERLOCKS

Although they are uncommon in gyms, holds that require hand jams and finger-locks are an important part of a climber's repertoire of grips. Hand jams work by placing your hand into a crack vertically and then maximizing the thickness of your hand in the crack so that the pressure created against the inside of the crack is enough to keep your hand secure. If the crack is perfectly symmetrical (does not narrow or widen), place your entire hand inside, with the thumb pointing up. From this position, slide your thumb down across the palm of your hand, so it's pointing down. This shift increases the thickness of your hand in the crack and secures your grip. Pressure must be maintained or your hand will slip out of the crack. Constricting hand jams, those that are narrower at the bottom than the top, are more secure, as the hand can be "slotted" down until tight. Hand jams can be done with the hand facing either up or down.

Fingerlocks are similar to hand jams. When the crack is so narrow that you cannot slide your hand into it, use just your fingers instead. The fingertips are placed into the crack as far as they will go, then the palm is twisted down to lock the fingers into place. Hand jams and fingerlocks are not the most comfortable types of hand positions, especially without taping your hands, but they do have their time and place for successful climbing.

MATCHING HANDS AND FEET

You may find yourself in a position where you want to switch your hands or "match" both hands on a particular hold. If the hold is large enough, taking one hand off and replacing it with the other is not very difficult. With small holds, however, start by taking a few fingers off the hold at a time, and replace them with the fingers of your free hand. It also helps to make room for the match by providing space on the hold for the new hand. Since you can replace one finger at a time, matching hands is not nearly as difficult as matching feet.

Just as with sloping footholds, maximize surface area between the hands and the sloper. Here, Emily keeps her center of gravity low to pull down on a sloper.

KEY EXERCISE: LEARNING TO STAY IN BALANCE WHILE MAINTAINING AN EVEN DISTRIBUTION OF WEIGHT

Overgripping with the hands, unbalanced movement, and excessive stabilization from the upper body are all factors that contribute to jerky moves and fatigued climbing. Overcome these burdens by paying attention to the amount of force exerted in your grip, to whether or not you feel balanced, and to how much weight your arms are bearing.

The Goal: Learn to use light hands while climbing, keep movement balanced and stable, and maintain an even distribution of body weight.

The Setup: Find a route that you have comfortably climbed without falling. Be sure to go through the proper checks and commands with your belayer before climbing.

HAND/FOOT PAUSE EXERCISE

1. With every hand move, hover your hand a few inches from the hold for a count of three before grabbing it. In that pause, ask yourself:
    - Is my weight distributed over my feet?
    - Can I relax the grip I have on the other hold?
    - Take your time to be sure that you pause for every handhold.
2. After you have completed the climb, repeat the exercise. This time, hover your foot above each foothold instead of your hand. During the pause, ask yourself:
    - Can I put more weight on my standing foot?
    - Can I position my body to take more weight off my arms?

CONSIDERATIONS

- Do not get on climbs that are so difficult that you cannot pause.
- Pause with only your hands *or* your feet, not both. Combining the two of them into one exercise can be overwhelming and can produce robotic climbing.

When matching your feet on large holds, simply make enough room to place both feet on the hold. If you cannot get both feet on the hold, try rolling one foot off the hold and rolling the other foot onto the hold in the same smooth motion. This rolling technique is not as effective on tiny footholds and nubbins.

The hop-step method of exchanging feet is most commonly used on smaller footholds. With this method, place the free foot directly over the weighted foot.

An efficient foot-match sequence requires precision, patience, and plenty of practice. Stay focused on looking at your feet and the hold: a, Maintain pressure on the standing foot and position the inside edge of the free foot as close to the hold as possible; b, As you slowly roll the weighted foot off the hold, roll the free foot onto the hold at the same time; c, Now the previously weighted foot is free. It will take some practice to make this transition smooth.

KEY EXERCISE: LEARNING HOW TO EXCHANGE HANDS AND FEET ON HOLDS

There are often occasions when you want to replace either one hand or one foot with the other hand or foot on a hold. You may need to make the switch because you are out of sequence, or because the route requires switching out your hands or feet.

The Goal: Learn to make quick and smooth transitions when switching one hand or foot for the other.

The Setup: Position the handholds at about chest height and the footholds near the ground. Make sure the footholds provide a stable enough base for a comfortable stance. The holds should range from big enough for matching hands or feet easily to micro-sized.

SWITCH OUT EXERCISE
Hands
1. Start with a comfortable stance on the footholds, with one hand on a handhold.
2. Practice taking one hand off the hold while putting the other one on. Take your time when taking your fingers off, and try to make room for the new hand.
3. As you feel more comfortable and the movement becomes smoother, move on to progressively smaller holds.

Feet
1. Stand with one foot on the largest foothold. Grab handholds that allow for the most comfortable body position.
2. Replace your standing foot with your free foot using the following methods:
   - Foot roll
   - Hop-step
   - Smearing
3. Move on to progressively smaller holds as your technique improves.

CONSIDERATIONS
- Be creative with hand positions to make room for switching out your hands. Consider pinching different parts of the hold or stacking one hand on top of the other. Vary the style of holds, using everything from slopers to pockets to edges.
- For the hop-step, position your free foot as close to your weighted foot as possible before switching feet. A lot of time and energy can be wasted trying to switch out your feet.
- Keep your arms straight while smearing.
- Practice the foot switches until you feel confident and smooth on even the smallest of holds.

It should hover mere centimeters over the supporting foot. In one smooth motion, pull the weighted foot out and step down with the free foot onto the hold. It takes a significant amount of practice to switch out your feet without scraping the wall with the stepping foot and to achieve a precise landing. When this move is performed quickly and efficiently, the upper body should have to take up very little additional weight.

The disadvantage of the hop-step is that you can never see the hold you are stepping on. You can only feel with the weighted foot and make a good estimate of what the hold is like. For micro-footholds, feel alone may be inadequate, and more precision may be needed. Switching your feet out by smearing is a more precise method than foot hopping. If you are standing on a hold with your left foot, smear your right foot against the wall near the hold, freeing up your left foot. Then, smear your left foot against the wall near the foothold. With both feet smearing for just a moment, you can then see the foothold and use pinpoint precision when placing your right foot on it. Because both feet are smearing for a moment, this technique puts more strain on the arms than the hop-step, but it allows for more precision.

CROSSING THROUGH

Once you have developed a keen sense of balance and footwork in the frontal position, it is time to focus on moving smoothly and efficiently. Climbers rarely ascend in a straight line, like people do a ladder. Even when you are climbing straight up, you often make subtle lateral movements. On the wall, these lateral movements can be made by sidestepping and then matching your feet. So far, our attention to weight shifting has been on this type of side-to-side movement, but sometimes you need to employ a different course of action.

From traversing to moving a few feet to the side, crossing through with your hands and feet is often more efficient than sidestepping. By crossing your hands and feet over each other, you can do half as many moves more fluidly.

If you are traveling to the left, rotate your upper body to face that direction. Rotate your right shoulder toward the wall and let your arm cross through to the left, between your body and the wall. Use the grasp of your right hand to help shift your weight over your left foot. Once your right foot is free, cross it through your body and place it to the left of your left foot. Follow that by releasing your left hand and reaching out to the next hold. After stepping out with your left foot again, you will be in your starting position.

Crossing through is never as easy as 1, 2, 3, but the idea is for hand and foot movements to complement each other. If you traverse too far with just your arms, your feet will be left behind and you will find yourself off balance and ready to "barn door," or swing, off the wall. Lead too far with your feet, and you will be in a tangled mess trying to get your upper body to follow. At times, you may have to match or interchange your hands or feet to stay in balance as you cross through.

KEY EXERCISE: LEARNING HOW TO MOVE LATERALLY BY CROSSING THROUGH

A climber rarely moves straight up. Ascending often requires some lateral movement. Although such movement may range from subtle moves to horizontal traverses, there are smoother and more effective ways to move sideways than by shuffling the hands and feet. Crossing the hands and feet between the climber's body and the wall is most effective.

The Goal: Learn to develop lateral movement skills that combine efficiency and smoothness.

The Setup: Set up the holds in a horizontal traverse with an assortment of grips. Put up more than are needed to allow for a variety of movements.

CROSS-THROUGH EXERCISE

1. Start by getting on the traverse to the right side.
2. Cross your right hand between your body and the wall, reaching to the left. Your right hip should be angled toward the wall and your upper body should be facing to the left.
3. Keep moving left by stepping through with your right foot.
4. Before stepping with your left foot in the same direction, be sure to shift your weight over your right foot.
5. Continue a combination of hand and foot cross-throughs until you reach the end of the traverse, and then head back to the start.

CONSIDERATIONS

- It may not be feasible to cross through with both your hands and feet for every move. Shuffling, matching, or switching out your hands or feet may be necessary at times to stay in balance.
- Try to stay upright throughout the exercise. Leading too far with your hands or feet will cause an imbalance in body positioning.
- As the traverse becomes smoother, limit the number of holds you use.
- Make the exercise more challenging by completing the entire traverse with as few foot- and handholds as possible.

Although the move is described as crossing through with hands and feet, the climber initiates and maintains the movement from his core. By leading with his hips, Matt can more easily move his hands and feet across his body: a, Before moving his right hand across his body, he keeps his left arm straight, maximizing efficiency. Because he'll be moving to the left, he keeps his right hip positioned close to the wall to help initiate the cross; b, As he crosses his right arm left, he gently rotates his hips to help drive his right arm left; c, To continue to move to the left, Matt has to unwind his body and reach up with his left hand.

KEY EXERCISE: LEARNING TO MOVE DYNAMICALLY FROM BAD HOLDS

Climbers are not always strong enough or in the right body position to securely grab on to holds and maintain control. At these times, momentum-based dynamic movement is the preferred technique in making further progress.

The Goal: Learn to move dynamically off a poorly gripped hold to another hold.

The Setup: Position several footholds near the ground. The handholds should be placed so that there are both positive and difficult-to-grab handholds on either side of your body. At your midline, place a decent handhold within reach above your head.

GOOD-HOLD/BAD-HOLD EXERCISE

1. Step onto the footholds in a comfortable stance, and grab a good hold with your right hand and a poor hold with your left.
2. Prepare to move your right hand on the good hold up to the other hold above your head. Your left hand will remain on the bad hold during the movement.
3. Before you move your right hand, center your gravity over your feet.
4. Once centered, use your legs to push your hips up and toward the targeted hold.
5. As your hips start to slow from the upward momentum you have created, quickly move your right hand to the hold.
6. Be prepared to control your momentum as soon as you latch on to the desired hold.
7. Continue the exercise by starting over and switching hands.

CONSIDERATIONS

Depending on the amount of balance you can maintain from weighting your feet, and the distance to the targeted hold, the momentum from your hips can range from a subtle shift in your hips (by pushing slightly with your legs) to more dramatic movement initiated from your legs and requiring you to pull with the good hold.

Opposite: *Tactics for bad holds: a, As the climber sets up for the move, notice how her hips and center of gravity are low, to help keep pressure on the handholds; b, Once the movement is initiated, her hips and center of gravity are moving in the direction she wants her hand to travel. She uses momentum to carry her hips upward and quickly move her left hand up. As you feel more comfortable with this movement, choose more challenging holds.*

DYNAMIC MOVEMENT

All the movement described in this chapter thus far pertains to static movement. Since static movement is more controlled than dynamic movement, it is often the preferred method of movement. However, static movement limits holds to those within your reach, which are determined by your strength, body positioning, and balance. Momentum-based dynamic moves are often the only choice in extending your reach or making an off-balance move. They can be performed as subtle "deadpoints" to holds a few inches away or as all-points-off-the-wall "dynos" to holds several feet away.

DEADPOINTS

Imagine that you are on a vertical wall, standing on decent footholds. Your right hand is on a secure hold and your left is on a poorly sloping hold that you cannot hold on to very well. You do not have the strength or body positioning to allow you to take control of the left-hand sloper and reach up with your right hand. In this case, a momentum-based deadpoint is the solution.

If a ball were thrown up into the air, it would eventually slow down to the point where it would momentarily stop in midair, and then travel back down to the earth. The apex of its flight is the deadpoint, or the point at which there is no movement. To apply that to our climbing scenario, you want to move your body toward the hold with enough momentum that when you reach your deadpoint, the hold is close enough to grab. Because momentum is carrying you toward the desired hold, your left hand does not require full control of the bad sloper.

The key to all dynamic movement is to initiate movement from the hips. If you can get your center of gravity traveling, you can decrease the distance between your

PUTTING ON YOUR DYNAMIC GAME F.A.C.E.

There are four crucial steps to making effective dynamic movements while climbing: focus, aim, commit, and execute.

1. **Focus:** Focus your attention on the task at hand. If you are a static climber or are not comfortable with dynamic moves, take time to psychologically adjust to a shift in your movement.
2. **Aim:** Take a good look at your target. Decide which hand to reach with and what part of the hold to grab. As you travel toward the hold, your perspective of the target will change, so keep it locked in your sights.
3. **Commit:** Before you complete the move, release yourself from reservations and give yourself the confidence you need to follow through.
4. **Execute:** You cannot just sit there all day planning the move. Know that you have taken a logical approach to the move, and it's time to fly.

With his hands and feet completely off the wall, Matt is fully committed to this move. Complete focus on the target hold is necessary to snatch it.

reaching hand and the hold. The common mistake climbers make with dynamic moves is reaching with their arms instead of with their hips. Reaching with the hands too early in a dynamic move causes the hips to move away from the wall to counterbalance the reach.

In a perfect deadpoint, the hips are pushed toward the desired hold. This is done with the legs, and the arms provide secondary support in the movement. As soon as the hips have reached their apex, the reaching hand moves toward the hold, continuing the momentum of the movement. As soon as you grab the desired hold, be prepared to stabilize your body. The momentum you have created must eventually be controlled.

DYNOS

Dynos are exaggerated deadpoints. The most extreme dynos require the climber to completely leave contact with the wall, travel through the air, and latch on to another hold. The same principles of deadpoint movement still apply.

KEY EXERCISE: LEARNING TO DYNO FAR DISTANCES

Sometimes holds are simply out of reach statically. However, with a lot of commitment and some momentum, bridging long gaps of several feet between holds is possible.

The Goal: To perform dynos with one and two hands through momentum-based movement.

The Setup: Position a hold large enough for both hands at about chest height. Set up a vertical line of a few large handholds starting a bit higher than head height. Set up the footholds in a few horizontal lines below the starting handhold, giving multiple options for height.

When practicing dynos, start with short movements to get comfortable with timing. Gradually practice on holds farther and farther away.

THE TWO-HANDED DYNO EXERCISE

Although starting with two-handed dynos may be more difficult than one-handed dynos, it is a more effective way to reinforce the technique.

1. Grab the starting hold with both hands, and sink your hips low so your arms are straight. Your hips should be square with the wall and your toes set so there is at least a 90-degree bend in your knees.
2. To initiate the dyno, drive your hips up the wall toward the target by pushing with your legs. Your arms should pull your body in toward the wall.
3. When your hips start to slow down, reach with both hands to the targeted hold.
4. As you feel more comfortable, target the progressively higher holds on the wall.

THE ONE-HANDED DYNO EXERCISE

This is not much different than the above exercise. In this case, only one hand reaches for the targeted hold.

1. Grab the starting hold with both hands, and sink your hips low until your arms are straight.
2. Decide which hand you are going to reach with. You may want to angle your hips so that the side of your body that you are reaching with is toward the wall. This twisting position can give you some extra extension.
3. To initiate the dyno, drive your hips up the wall toward the target by pushing with your legs. Your arms should pull your body in toward the wall.
4. If your hips are angled at all, the driving upward force will come from the leg that is closest to the wall.
5. Because the hand that remains on the starting hold is stable as the other hand reaches through the air, it is difficult to let go with that hand at the end of the move. To facilitate letting go of the first hold, think of pushing off that stable hand at the end of the move.
6. As you feel more comfortable, target the progressively higher holds on the wall.

CONSIDERATIONS

- Performing this exercise on a top-rope climb is not recommended. It is difficult for a belayer to take up slack when the climber is performing long dynos, and there is the possibility of getting the rope wrapped around the hand midflight.
- A competent spotter is needed for this exercise in order to minimize the risk of the climber falling back if the targeted hold is missed. Spotting is discussed in detail in Chapter 4, Bouldering.
- Momentum must be maintained through the lower body driving the hips up. Extension can be made all the way down through the toes.
- Do not forget to put on your dyno F.A.C.E.!

To set up for a dyno, get your feet high and underneath you if possible. The higher your feet, the more you can push off, and the closer they are to the desired target. Often, a pumping action with the hands and feet is helpful to develop some initial momentum and position the hips over the feet. Once you are ready to fly, explode by pushing with your feet when your hips are over them. Counteract the tendency to push the body away from the wall by using your hands to pull yourself in toward the wall.

Just like deadpoints, delay reaching with your hands for the target until your momentum is starting to slow down. Reach too early, and you may lose all your momentum. Though reaching with one hand to the target allows the other hand to stay on the starting hold for longer, latching on with one hand can be difficult after such a long move. If the target hold is big enough, consider a double-handed approach. The commitment level is higher, but it's much easier to regain control with two hands than one.

SEQUENCING

More a mental aspect of climbing than a physical technique, sequencing is the most significant factor in smoothly stringing individual moves together. It is the ability to look at a route and determine what moves to do and how to do them, from finding the starting holds to determining what direction the climb travels. If you aimlessly grab holds, you are less likely to find yourself climbing the route's path of least resistance.

Sequencing enables you to make fewer moves and achieve better body positioning, as well as anticipate difficult or confusing sections of the route and identify easy sections for rests. The four main approaches to sequencing are the preclimb (from the ground up), while climbing, after falling, and after climbing.

PRECLIMB
The preclimb sequence, also known as ground-up sequencing, takes place before you actually climb the route. Try to gather as much information as possible about the route. Identify the general direction of the climb, find all the holds, and locate any natural features, such as corners. Also, identify difficult sections that you may have a hard time with, and look for easier sections where you can rest. Take note of any potential technical hazards, like big top-rope swings or tricky lead climbing clips.

WHILE CLIMBING
Once you have gathered the big picture and begin climbing, in-climb sequencing allows you to anticipate moves up to four or five holds in front of you. If you focus on too much of the route, like the anchors, it is easy to miss holds in your immediate reach. Conversely, too much attention paid to the holds within your grasp can lead you astray. If your pre- and in-climb sequencing skills and climbing technique come together well enough, then you will find yourself at the anchors, having successfully completed your climb.

Having just fallen, Emily takes the opportunity to figure out a more efficient sequence that will maximize her friction on difficult holds.

AFTER FALLING AND AFTER CLIMBING

Yes, at some point you will fall on a route. Try not to feel defeated. Instead, take the opportunity to figure out if there are any technical alternatives to the sequence you just fell from. Before jumping back on the route, since you're already hanging on the rope, look around—perhaps there are holds you did not see or use.

Get back on the route a few moves lower than where you fell and in the same sequence. From here, figure out a new way if need be. The idea is not to just get through the moves but to figure them out for future success.

As soon as you get off the route, mentally review the sequence to burn it into your memory. Figuring out the sequence postclimb is the same as preparing for the next preclimb sequencing on the same route.

A SOLID FOUNDATION

Now that you have learned the basics of weight shifting, footwork, body positioning, and movement, you can continue to apply these techniques to the key exercises presented in this chapter. As these exercises become more comfortable, focus on applying the techniques to more challenging routes. Keep practicing so that easy terrain feels easy! Even the most advanced and elite climbers have built this foundation. They now have the ability to instinctually adjust to varying terrain and situations.

Opposite: *Bouldering lends itself to explosive and difficult movement, right off the ground.*

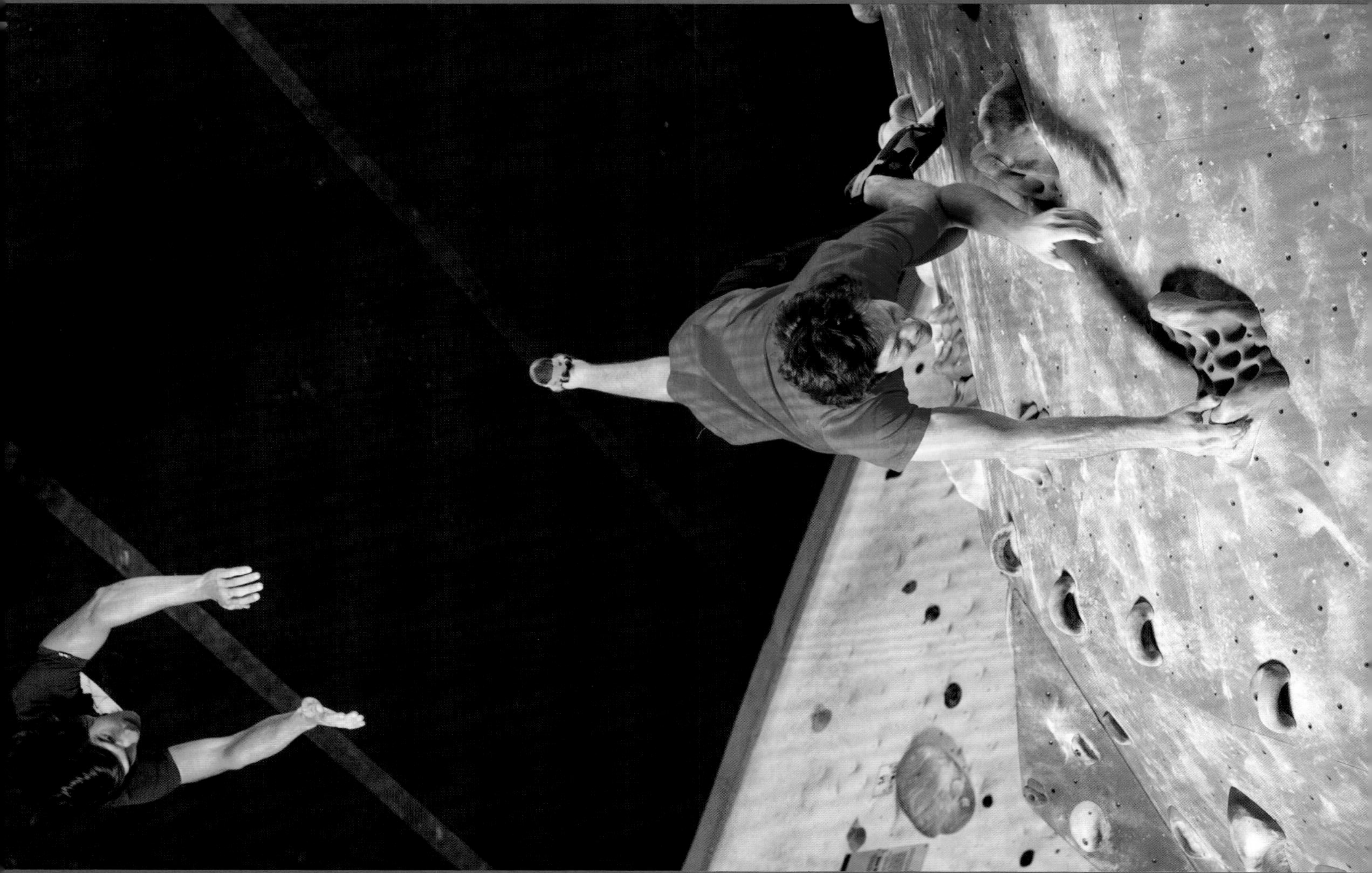

CHAPTER 4

Bouldering

One of the youngest disciplines of climbing, bouldering is growing up fast. Outdoor bouldering was once an activity that climbers did on rest days. Back then, it was absurd to think that climbers would want to spend their time tackling house-sized boulders. But the purity of bouldering, just the climber and rock, without extraneous gear to fumble with while climbing, has become the appeal. The hardest climbing moves done on the smallest holds have all happened on boulder routes, which are better known as problems. There are international outdoor climbing areas that attract only boulderers, gyms that offer only bouldering walls, and even companies that manufacture only bouldering gear and equipment.

A significant factor in bouldering's maturity is the social aspect. In roped climbing, it's just you and your belay partner. While bouldering, however, there's an awful lot of sitting around, cheering on your crew, spotting for safety, and helping each other figure out the "beta" (moves). While sport and trad climbers protect each other with a rope, boulderers provide safety with their bare hands by spotting each other when they fall off a problem.

Bouldering's physical appeal stems from its focus on movement, the little gear needed, its low barrier to entry, and the fact that it can be done solo. A boulder problem can range from a one-move wonder to a never-ending traverse. In the time spent on a problem, the climber is simply focused on the moves at hand. There are no distractions from a harness or rope, no fumbling with clipping or unclipping carabiners. Success or failure on a boulder problem is often measured by subtle changes in body positioning.

Because of the minimal requirements for safety and performance equipment in bouldering, including the fact that the boulderer does not need a belayer, a beginner can start bouldering within minutes of being introduced to the activity. There are no knots to learn or formal commands to remember—just you and the wall. However, a new boulderer should be well informed of the risks that come with bouldering. Because of the freedoms that bouldering offers, there are compromises in safety compared to top-rope climbing.

Another advantage that bouldering has over climbing routes is the actual amount of climbing that can fit into a given amount of time. A proficient duo of top-rope climbers may get in a half dozen routes apiece in an hour, whereas a boulderer could theoretically climb nonstop in that same amount of time.

Because bouldering is such an intense form of climbing, relatively good rest holds and positions are rare on set boulder problems. Indoor bouldering is also characterized by overhanging walls. These features put more of the climber's weight on the upper body, creating extremely difficult moves on still-decent holds.

Bouldering may best be described as free-form gymnastics performed on rock faces. The rock provides features, and the climber must create a routine to match those features. The physical and mental demands of the two activities have similarities as well. Participants must be able to blend technical skill with strength and balance while maintaining the mental edge for success and safety.

GETTING STARTED

Bouldering can be intimidating. Climbers swinging through the air or falling out of the sky, the steep terrain, and the absence of a top rope can make a bouldering area seem foreign to any climber, new or experienced. If the crowds are intimidating, consider bouldering at off-peak hours, such as a weekday afternoon. You will likely have the gym to yourself. At the same time, it's true that there is safety in numbers, so try to recruit your climbing partner to go bouldering with you, or meet up with some more-experienced friends so they can show you the ropes, so to speak.

WHAT TO CLIMB

A beginner should focus on horizontal traverses, as opposed to vertical problems. This way, novices can pay attention to their movement, and the ground remains only a short step away. Boulderers with more experience may want to scope out problems that look interesting and appropriate for their current ability. All climbers should choose a height that they feel comfortable falling or jumping down from. This may be the top of a problem for some climbers or just a few feet off the ground for others. If you have not properly warmed up yet, start with some very easy problems to stretch your muscles and tendons.

If there are too few routes set at your experience level, you may want to approach the ones available with some modifications. To make established routes climbable, consider using all the footholds on the wall while sticking to the marked handholds. This approach allows you the freedom to place your feet on the most efficient holds for your body type and to maintain proper body positioning. As your bouldering ability improves, try to stay on the designated footholds.

With the bouldering V scale, the higher the number, the more difficult the problem.

RATINGS

Because boulder problems are much shorter than roped routes, a lot of punch is packed into a little bit of climbing. Roped routes are rated on the Yosemite Decimal System (YDS), a subjective scale of difficulty, based on the hardest moves, or "crux," of the climb. Bouldering focuses on difficulty: it packs the hardest part of route climbing into a few moves right off the ground. Because of this difference, bouldering has its own grading system. And while it is possible to convert between the bouldering V scale and the YDS, the individual moves that elite boulderers perform are often more difficult than what elite route climbers execute.

As the grading comparison scale in the next chapter shows, the V scale does not extend below the YDS grade of 5.8 because the nature of bouldering is climbing difficult moves. The discrepancy becomes apparent when bouldering at the V0 grade. A boulder problem of this grade can reflect the hardest moves of a YDS climb ranging from 5.0 to 5.7. Some gyms have created their own sub-V0 scale to help climbers choose routes that are more appropriate for their level.

Some gyms choose to not use the V scale to rate their problems and use their own system. Sometimes they're color coded, with each color representing a "range" within the V scale. For instance, green problems may cover an "intermediate" range of V3–V5, and so on. Whatever scale a gym uses, it's important to understand that ratings are all relative. Moves that may seem hard to you may play to your weaknesses, and a problem that seems easy may fit your strengths.

SAFETY

An indoor climber is more likely to be injured from a bouldering fall than from a roped fall. When climbing on a rope, falls are protected by the rope, preventing the climber from hitting the ground. However, with bouldering, every fall—planned or not—results in the climber hitting the ground. Landing off balance can twist or sprain knees, ankles, or wrists. Just being in a bouldering cave increases your risk of injury, because another climber may fall on you. Having a flying boulderer land on you is no fun.

The appeal of bouldering indoors is the same as it is for roped climbing. The landing zones in outdoor areas will never be as flat or as cushioned as in a climbing gym, nor will emergency assistance be as close. Even with these controlled features, injury is always possible. In an effort to help minimize the risk of injury, consider the following guidelines:

1. Keep bottles and gear away from landing zones.
2. Be aware of your surroundings as a climber and as a spectator.
3. Know your limits.
4. Use a spotter.
5. Learn to fall, because you will.
6. Be prepared to hit the ground every time you fall.
7. Take responsibility for your own safety.

FOLLOWING A PROBLEM

Designated bouldering areas and caves are often riddled with holds and have a rainbow of tape or colored holds on the wall marking set routes. Check with the gym staff to see if the colors have any specific meaning. There is usually a descriptive note at the beginning of the problem that may indicate the grade, a name for identification, and any other pertinent information. The starts of boulder problems are like those of roped routes: hands should start on a specific hold.

A boulder problem that is set to be climbed by tracking means that the hand- and footholds marked with one tape color are the only ones you can use to complete the problem at the given grade. Any other hand- or foothold is not considered a part of the route. Of course, you can always disregard the established problems and climb on whatever looks like fun, or perhaps just stick to the designated handholds and use any footholds. Remember, climbing is what you make of it.

FINISHING

The top, or finish, of a boulder problem is designated with either a finish hold (the last marked hold) or a climb up and over the top of the wall, which is known as

A boulder problem is complete when the climber either grabs the last handhold or the top of the wall (as shown here) or stands on top of the boulder.

topping out. With a designated finish hold, simply grab it and you're done. If there's a lip on the top of the wall, that acts as the finishing hold. Some bouldering areas are designed for you to climb onto the top of the wall, like you would a boulder outside—this topping-out technique is discussed later in this chapter.

GETTING DOWN

What goes up must come down, and one aspect of safety is knowing the ways to get down from a bouldering problem. The safest way to descend is by climbing all the way back down to the ground. If you are climbing at your limit, this may be a problem since you have spent all your energy on the ascent. Look for the biggest holds you can reach, and use them to down-climb. Thoughtful climbing gyms place descent jugs on high bouldering walls.

Jumping down and falling are also options for descent but might not be wise from the top of tall bouldering walls. The difference between the two is that jumping down is a conscious decision and falling is not. When jumping down, check your landing zone. Hopefully, it is a clear area that is at a comfortable distance. If not, down-climb a bit, or traverse over to a bouldering pad. When jumping, avoid any rotation to prevent excess torque on your ankles or knees at impact. When landing, bend your legs slightly and land with both feet at the same time, and let your legs bend some more to absorb the force of the landing. On long-air-time jumps, continue your momentum to carry your upper body all the way down to the ground by rolling sideways.

Note that if you always revert to jumping or down-climbing when the moves get difficult, you will have a hard time pushing yourself and bettering your bouldering skills. Knowing how to fall will provide a comfort level that will let you push your limits.

When you push your personal performance envelope, you may fall at unexpected movements, due to how intently you are focusing on the movement at hand. After you realize you are falling, try to position your feet below your body, feet landing first and knees slightly bent, just like jumping down. Try to minimize rotation before you hit the ground. Be careful using your hands for stabilization once you hit the ground. Wrist sprains are a common injury when falling backward, since a natural reaction is to place your hands behind you to break the fall.

HITTING THE GROUND

You can minimize the risk of injury during a fall by employing some simple techniques upon landing and by having a spotter facilitate your landing. Both require practice to master and are instrumental in bouldering safely.

FALLING

Every time you fall while bouldering, you will hit the ground, sometimes with a significant amount of force. There's a high risk of injury when this happens if you're not prepared. Because the legs can absorb a lot of impact when you hit the ground, try to land with your ankles directly over your feet to prevent rolling an ankle. Absorb the force of the fall by bending your legs once your feet hit the ground (again, still maintaining your center of gravity over your legs). As your legs absorb the fall, roll backward onto the flooring. As you're rolling, tucking your chin will help stabilize your neck to prevent any whiplash.

No two falls are the same, and even a short fall can have consequences. Avoid

How to fall: a, As the boulderer falls to the ground, she keeps her feet under her to land with an equal distribution of weight on her feet; b, She uses her legs to absorb the shock of the fall; c, To disperse the force, she rolls onto her back; d, Notice how she avoids hitting the ground with her hands or wrists, which are commonly injured during a fall.

FALLING CHECKLIST
- Be aware of your landing zone.
- Bend your knees to absorb the force of the landing.
- Land on both feet.
- Keep your arms close to your body.
- Roll upon impact to absorb the fall.

landing on one leg or sticking an arm out to the side or back, both of which increase your risk of injuring your ankle, knee, wrist, elbow, or shoulder. If you anticipate landing on your hand, making a fist can combat hyperextending the wrist. Proper falling can limit injury to such an extent that many climbing and bouldering gyms conduct falling tests, similar to belay tests, before participants can boulder.

SPOTTING

Gymnasts use spotters during their routines to help safely guide them to the mats in a fall or dismount. Boulderers employ the same tactic since there is minimal protection from a fall. Being a spotter comes with the same responsibilities as being a belayer. The climber trusts you to have the focus and attention to react quickly and the technical skills to perform your duty properly. Being a good spotter can sometimes seem more difficult than being a good belayer due to distractions from other people around you, feeling excited for the boulderer, and not being physically linked to the climber

with a rope. Keep in mind, too, that as a spotter, you are at risk of injury just as much as the boulderer you are spotting.

The primary goal of the spotter is to help direct and slow the climber's fall. If the climber is merely stepping off the wall, the spotter helps the climber regain balance if necessary. However, a spiraling boulderer pitching from ten feet up may require the spotter to direct her toward a bouldering pad while righting her so her feet land first. A large part of directing a falling climber consists of the spotter protecting the climber's head, neck, and back by having her land feet first.

A secondary responsibility of the spotter is to make sure that the landing stays clear of obstacles and that the bouldering pads are moved according to where the climber might fall. But these tasks should be done only if they do not compromise the protection of a falling boulderer by taking the spotter's attention away. Obstacles should be cleared before the boulderer starts, and the spotter can direct mat placements to other people in the bouldering area.

The best positioning for a bouldering pad (or crash pad) ensures that the climber lands in the middle. Landing with one foot on the pad and one foot off results in an unbalanced impact and is a recipe for disaster. Additionally, the pad should always be moved smoothly. If the pad is moved with a strong jerk, and the climber falls and lands while the pad is still moving, he can bet on an ankle injury. When putting two pads together, diligently enforce a tight fit between the pads. Landing with a

Matt's athletic stance is ready to absorb the force of Emily's fall at any moment.

foot in the gap is another type of disastrous landing, which can easily twist an ankle or worse.

The ready position for spotting is an athletic stance with the legs shoulder-width apart or slightly wider. One foot can be in front of the other, with knees slightly bent to help either absorb the force of the climber or to help push for direction. Both arms should be raised and positioned near the climber's center of gravity. This position may range from the hips to the shoulders, depending on the climber's body type. The spotter should position his body between the climber and the ground. If the spotter is not standing close enough to the climber, the falling climber will simply slip through the spotter's arms. The spotter should keep his hands close enough together to prevent the boulderer's body from slipping through his hands. The spotter's hands should be positioned so the palms will take the brunt of the climber's force, with the thumbs kept tight to the hand to prevent sprains.

As the boulderer ascends, keep the hands raised and move accordingly. The steeper the climb, the more probable it is that a falling climber will be in a prone position while falling. Be ready to slow the climber down by contacting him slightly higher than his center of gravity, which will cause his legs to continue to fall and land sooner than his back and neck.

Just as belayers are ready to react to climbers from the moment they leave the ground until they return, spotters should never let their guard (or hands) down until the boulderer is safely on the ground. A common (and dangerous) mistake is to either stop spotting or let the hands down once the boulderer has reached the top of the climb. In fact, descending is one of the riskiest parts of any form of climbing. A hold could spin on the wall, or the climber could lose her balance and come crashing off the wall. As a spotter, dedicate your full attention for the duration of the ascent and descent.

Consider using multiple spotters for high-risk bouldering, even in the gym. Bouldering is a very social activity and there are often able bodies to help spot or move bouldering pads. Just make sure that everyone is an experienced spotter. An ineffective spotter is worse than none at all because it gives the climber a false sense of security, and poor spotting may injure the climber, himself, or other spotters.

SPOTTING CHECKLIST

- Keep your thumbs pressed against your hand and your stance athletic.
- Maintain a clean landing zone for your climber.
- Keep others from walking into the landing.
- Stay vigilantly focused on your climber.
- Make contact at the climber's center of gravity.

Effective spotting: a, Emily has her hands raised in anticipation of Matt's fall; b, She makes contact with Matt at his hips and waist, which allows her to break the initial impact of his fall.

ADVANCED TECHNIQUES

Due to the short bursts of power and high-intensity climbing required on boulder problems, the movement characteristics of bouldering can differ from roped climbing. All the climbing techniques described in Chapter 3, Movement Technique, are applicable to bouldering, but more advanced overhanging techniques like twistlocks and drop-knee moves are discussed below. Because many of these techniques require full-body involvement, core body strength is especially important in bouldering.

Core strength is defined as the ability to stabilize and control the stomach, lower back, and hips. Steep climbing depends on body positioning and hip placement, and core strength is the connector between tension created in the upper and lower body. The connection between upper-body tension, core tension, and lower-body tension is collectively called body tension. On vertical or less-than-vertical terrain, a climber's center of gravity pulls the hips into the feet. On steep overhanging terrain, where the climber is in a more horizontal position, gravity pulls the climber's hips down and away from the feet. Steep climbing and bouldering requires more body tension than vertical routes, and a climber needs a strong core to generate that level of body tension.

TWISTLOCKS

Overhanging terrain can be intimidating. However, with some changes in body position and technique, steep terrain can be masterfully climbed with grace and fluidity over brute strength and power. The most basic technique for steep climbing is the twistlock. The twistlock is a modification of crossing through. If you were to tackle an overhanging wall in a frontal position with your hips and chest square to the wall, gravity would tug your hips down and an incredible amount of force would be required from one arm to allow the other to simply let go and reach up. Although the principle of keeping as much weight over the feet as possible remains true, it must be achieved differently on an overhanging wall by using twistlocks.

To get a feel for the move, set up for a twistlock by sitting on the ground with your feet in front of you like they are on the wall and your hands out in front of your face like they are grabbing imaginary holds. Pretend you are on a 45-degree overhanging wall. To reach your right hand to a hold, drop your right knee toward the ground between your legs. You should feel your right hip lift off the ground, raising your right hand a bit higher in turn. This is the twisting motion of a twistlock. By dropping your knee, you have moved your center of gravity (hips) slightly closer to your feet and extended your reach by rotating your body. The final part comes from locking off the left arm by bending it just enough for the right hand to grab the hold.

Performing a twistlock is a full-body move. Your toes, fingertips, and everything in between are fully engaged to create enough body tension to keep your hips tight and prevent any body part from sagging. Since every body part has its job in performing an efficient twistlock, mastering this move takes a lot of practice, concentration, and body awareness.

It is important to use the inside edge of your toes when setting your feet up prior to a twistlock. This enables your body to pivot on your feet for a sufficient twist of the hips once the movement is engaged. The width of your stance also plays an important role in the line between balance and reach. If your feet are wide apart, you can generally maintain a more stable stance. The drawback is that your reach is compromised. Keeping your feet close together gives you maximum height when reaching, but the balance platform is less stable. Of course, the actual available footholds will dictate your stance, but when practicing twistlocks, experiment with different distances between your feet.

Also, it is imperative to keep your arms straight between twistlocks. If your elbow is bent, then the muscles in your arm are

Twistlock sequence (above): a, On the steep terrain shown in these two sequences, Emily keeps her arms as straight as possible; b, The "reaching" motion comes from her rotation of her hips and her "reaching" from her shoulders. Twistlock sequence (below): a, Emily engages her core to maintain body tension and keep her feet on the wall; b, Maintaining tension allows her to move her right arm up and across her body to the next positive hold.

contracted, taking the brunt of your weight. That is a sure way to tire quickly. If your arms are straight, the force of your weight is taken by the bones in your arms, rather than the muscles.

To reach with your right hand, engage the twist by rotating your right knee between your legs. This action will push your hip toward the wall. A narrow stance may require only a subtle swivel of your knee to get your hips in place, but a wide stance may require your knee to rotwate inward until it is pointed at the ground, flexibility permitting. Once you are twisted, concentrate on pushing your feet out from each other against the holds, rather than straight down. The more you push with your feet, the less body weight your arms feel. Moving up the body, keep your hips tight against the wall. In our example of reaching with the right hand, your right hip should be right up against, if not touching, the wall. Any relaxation in your abdomen will cause your hips to sag from the wall, making it harder to maintain body positioning.

Your left arm should remain straight for as long as possible. When you move your right hand up, reach with your shoulders. Your left arm should remain stationary with a bend at your shoulder and with your right shoulder reaching for the next hold. The last movement in the twistlock is to break your weighted arm at the elbow if you need some extra extension to grab the hold.

When stringing together multiple twist-locks, keep your right arm straight as you weight it. Then, release the lower-body twist, and move your feet up the wall. You are now in the starting position for twist-locking on the other side of your body.

DROP-KNEE MOVES

Extreme twistlocks require the rotating knee to turn so severely that it can even point down and away from the wall. The benefit of this type of move is to maximize the pressure of the legs pushing out from each other and widen the climber's base of stability. Because of the high torque placed on the ligaments of the knee, this move has a high potential for knee injury. Although the move is quite effective, take care in executing big drop-knee moves.

This wall feature is extremely steep. To help Matt release his left hand to reach up, he turns his left hip toward the wall and points his knee toward the ground (hence the name "drop knee"). From this position, he can push his feet away from each other, removing weight from his arms.

By slotting her right knee behind a hold and keeping her right foot flexed to maintain tension, Emily has found a creative no-hands rest, a knee bar, in the middle of a problem.

HEEL AND TOE HOOKS

The key to climbing steep overhangs is to weight the lower body as much as possible to avoid straining the arm muscles too much. Heel and toe hooks are effective ways of shifting your weight to your lower body. These moves allow the lower body to pull instead of push. Heel hooks are most effective when placed in a horizontal line with the hands. Although this requires a certain amount of flexibility, it essentially creates a third hanging point, in addition to the arms. When moving from this position, forcefully pull the hips toward the heel hook with the hamstring muscles. Raising the hips high minimizes the distance the arm needs to reach to grasp the next handhold.

A solid toe hook can also pull the center of gravity over the feet more effectively. Pay special attention to keeping the

To generate the most power out of this right heel hook, Emily pulls her heel toward her right hip, leveraging her weight over the heel.

hooking foot and ankle rigid as the toes and hips are pulled together. A toe hook can be secured by pushing the opposite foot on the same hold. Referred to as a bicycle move, this pushing of the opposite foot and pulling of the toes allow the lower body to lock into the hold.

MANTLING

At first, topping out on a boulder problem can leave you feeling like a beached whale—with flailing arms and legs trying to get over the bulge of a bouldering wall. But a proper mantle—pushing down on the top of a boulder until your hips are high enough to step your feet next to your hands—can look and feel like getting out of the deep end of a pool. At some point, there won't be any more holds to "pull down" on, and you'll have to rely on shifting your center of gravity over your feet and standing up. A common technique is to

The key to smooth mantling and topping out is to maintain contact with your hands and feet rather than using elbows or knees. As Matt rocks his weight over his right foot, he'll be able to stand up and push with his legs, instead of pulling with his arms.

KEY EXERCISE: LEARNING MOVEMENT BY BOULDERING WITH OTHER CLIMBERS

In roped climbing, there is seldom the chance to climb with more than one other person at a time. Bouldering reveals a more social aspect of climbing and allows multiple participants to climb with, learn from, and help each other. This group game enforces sequencing, visualization, and movement, all on steep terrain in a bouldering environment.

The Goal: Learn to develop sequencing and visualization skills, hold memorization, and hold selection through a group bouldering game.

The Setup: The bouldering wall should be set with a wide variety of hand- and footholds. There do not need to be any set bouldering problems.

ADD-ON EXERCISE

1. The first boulderer starts by choosing and climbing three moves on the wall.
2. The next climber must climb using the same three holds as the first climber, then add three more moves of her own.
3. The next climber performs the previous six moves, and then adds three more.
4. When all the climbers have gone, the cycle repeats with the first climber again.
5. When a climber fails to repeat all the moves and add three more, he is out. The next climber attempts the same moves.
6. The game continues until one person is left climbing.

CONSIDERATIONS

- Gauge the ability of the group. Adding moves that are too hard for most of the climbers does not make the game fun for everyone.
- Determine what the goal of the game is before you start. If it is a game of endurance, keep the moves easy and flowing. Training for power will keep the number of moves short.
- The more people playing, the more quickly the problem will grow longer. Consider adding only two or even one move if you have a lot of climbers.

Opposite: *The positive energy and shared feedback from working on a problem with another boulderer can help push you out of your own comfort zone.*

push down on the handholds as your raise your center of gravity and hike your feet up (just as you might push down on the edge of a pool with your hands and bring a foot up next to them to get out). Tricky boulder problems may not have any handholds on top, and you'll have to resort to holding on to the lip of the climbing wall with your hands and perhaps smearing your feet as you get higher. Smooth, fluid movements and a bit of commitment will help you hone your indoor mantling technique.

REMEMBER SAFETY

As noted before, every time you let go of the wall while bouldering, you will hit the ground at a speed relative to your height on the wall. If you are near the ground, the fall should not be a problem, but coming off the wall at fourteen feet poses very different risks, even with a team of experienced spotters. Since you are responsible for your own safety, it is important for you to know your limits. Only you know what you are capable (and incapable) of doing. Never assume that someone will spot you. Ask for a spot from someone proficient every time you think you may need one. While spotting is deeply ingrained in the outdoor bouldering community, it is not as much a part of the indoor culture due to the level and softly padded flooring.

Move the crash pads into an anticipated landing zone. If possible, cover the entire area below the climb. If that is not possible, pad the area below the crux or the higher, more potentially dangerous parts of the problem. Anticipate moves that may carry you away from the wall, like long dynos or sideways lunges. Even with a perfect spotter, you can still get hurt.

A CULTURE IN ITSELF

Many climbers consider bouldering the "freest" expression of climbing. With no ropes, harnesses, or hardware, the focus is on climbing movement. In recent years, an overwhelming number of climbers have begun bouldering exclusively, with no desire to even get on a rope. With its dynamic nature, group mentality, and opportunity to get a lot of climbing done in a short amount of time, bouldering has tremendous appeal, and you can spend a lifetime enjoying this discipline without ever even roping up.

Opposite: *Top-rope climbing will get you off the ground and let you reach new heights.*

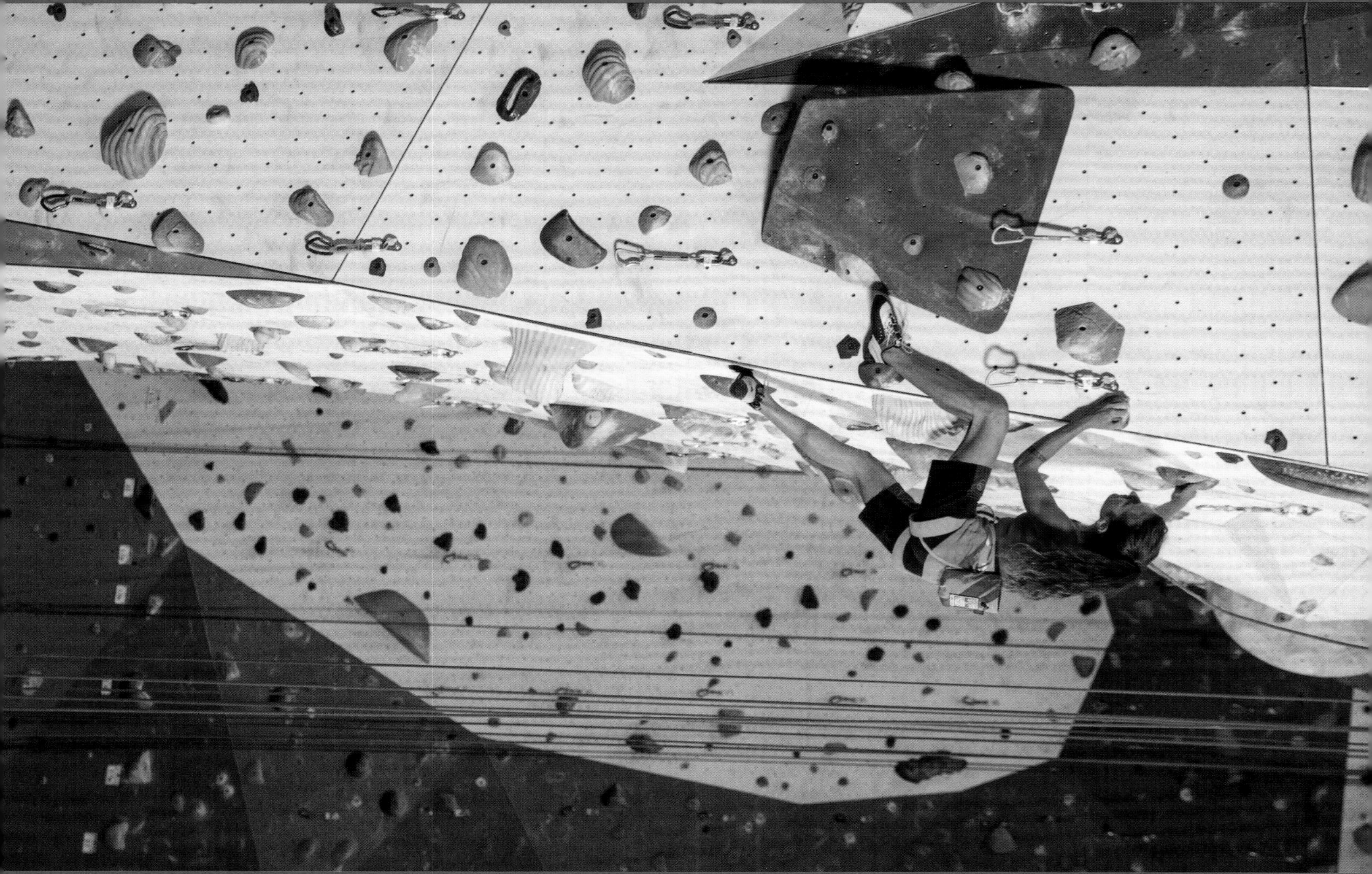

CHAPTER 5

Top-Rope Climbing

If you want to leave the bouldering area and venture to higher ground in the gym, top-roping is the next step. Top-rope climbs in a gym are set up as "slingshot" systems. The climber ties in to one end of a rope that runs up to an anchor and then back down to the belayer positioned on the ground. The belayer takes in rope as the climber ascends and keeps the rope from moving in the event of a fall. When the climber is ready to lower from the route, which can be done at any time, the belayer allows rope to slide through the belay device and controls the climber's speed of descent. Because the belayer is in control of all the rope work, the climber can focus on scaling the wall. Since the belayer needs to understand (and sometimes anticipate) the needs of the climber, a new student should start with climbing instruction before moving to belay instruction.

GETTING STARTED

In the gym, more than one route often shares space on the wall. The differentiation between routes is typically marked by different colored handholds, or grips. If you want to climb a specific route, that route is designated with the same color of holds. In a lesser-used method of identifying routes, the same colored tape is applied to the wall by each hold. Over time, the tape loses its stickiness and wears off.

Each route is labeled with a grade near the first handhold of the climb. To climb the described grade, use only the hand- and footholds identified for that route. Using additional holds may make the climb easier, but the idea of marked routes is to use the designated hand- and footholds while climbing. Other information may appear next to the starting hold, such as wall features that are on or off route, designated footholds, the name of the route for identification purposes, the route setter's name, or the date it was set.

GRADES

When starting out, most climbers tackle whatever looks fun to them rather than follow a prescribed route, grabbing any and all holds available to get to the top. This type of climbing can be fun at first, but there is more to climbing than just conquering the wall and getting to the top. After a few climbs of grabbing any hold available, understanding the grading scale can help new climbers learn what routes are considered challenging and why.

Climbs are rated on the Yosemite Decimal System (YDS), and roped climbs are considered fifth-class climbs, designated with the prefix 5. A fall from a fifth-class route while climbing without a rope can be fatal. The other categories, first class through fourth class, refer to outdoor terrain ranging from hiking to scrambling with the hands and feet with or without a rope.

A gym route rating may or may not have the prefix 5 but will always include another set of numbers, and perhaps a letter or a plus or minus sign. The numbers following 5 represent the difficulty of the route. The scale is open ended, but it starts at 1 and currently reaches 15. For grades above 10, the difficulty beaks down further in ascending order from *a* through *d*. For example, a 5.11b would be read "five eleven b" and would be slightly more difficult than a 5.11a. Sometimes a plus or minus sign is used instead of the letter rating.

Novice climbers usually start in the 5.5 to 5.7 range. Climbing 5.12 and beyond is a considerable accomplishment, requiring a strong command of climbing technique, physical conditioning, and mental resolve. Right now, the upper echelon are climbing 5.15.

Several factors contribute to the subjective grade of a climb. The wall's terrain and the size, number, and spacing of the holds all affect the overall grade. In the gym, route setters create climbs based on their own experiences with rock climbing. Hard routes do not simply have fewer or smaller holds, but force the climber to use specific techniques. In fact, larger holds without a solid edge to grab are the most difficult to hold on to. Keep in mind that routes requiring long reaches for a short climber may be easier for a tall climber, and someone with smaller hands may find a climb easier (or harder) than someone with bigger hands.

Terrain, defined as the angle or steepness of the climbing surface, plays a significant role in the difficulty of the route. A less-than-vertical wall, or slab, leans away from you. With slabby terrain, you can keep your center of gravity over your feet and use your hands for balance, similar to the action of walking up stairs. Slabs are a good starting place for novice climbers since the upper body does not become as fatigued as it does in vertical or steep climbing. Vertical and near-vertical climbs are straight up and down, forcing

Route cards communicate details about a particular route or problem, like the grade, the date it was set, the name of the route setter, and even a name for the route or problem.

YOSEMITE DECIMAL SYSTEM VERSUS V SCALE

YDS	V SCALE	YDS	V SCALE
5.8	V0-	12d	V6
5.9	V0	13a	V7
10a	V0+	13b	V8
10b	V0+	13c	V9
10c	V1	13d	V9
10d	V1	14a	V10
11a	V2	14b	V11
11b	V2	14c	V12
11c	V3	14d	V13
11d	V3	15a	V14
12a	V4	15b	V15
12b	V4	15c	V16
12c	V5	15d	V17

the climber to engage the arms more than on a less-than-vertical wall. The most impressive climbs to watch (and climb) are on steep, overhanging walls. The difficulty of steep terrain lies in the advanced techniques necessary to keep the climber's weight over the feet and not have the upper body tire out too quickly.

The YDS scale is very different from the bouldering V scale described in the previous chapter, but a rough comparison can be made.

TYING IN

After determining which route to climb, find the appropriate rope to use. This should not be too confusing in a well-laid-out gym. The last hold of the route must be positioned near the top-rope anchors. If not, the potential swing of falling near the finish of the route can be dangerous.

Often, the climber and belayer must choose which end of the rope to tie in to and which end to belay from. The climber's end of the rope should travel to the nearest anchor point at the top of the climb. Avoid any tangles or twists around the ropes when setting up.

FIGURE-EIGHT FOLLOW-THROUGH

Also known as the figure-eight retrace, the figure-eight follow-through is the most widely used tie-in knot in gym climbing. The symmetrical pattern of the finished knot makes identification easy. If you're new to knot tying, check with your gym for

Often there is already a figure-eight knot tied into the climbing end of a rope in a gym, which you'll simply need to follow through, making five pairs of parallel strands of rope. If you need to tie the initial knot, follow this sequence: a, Start by pulling out an arm's length of rope; b, Make a loop in the rope, with the tail end on bottom; c, Wrap the tail end over the climbing strand (closer to you than the existing loop) to make an eight; d, Wrap the tail end under the climbing strand; e, Poke the tail through the first loop; f, Admire your work.

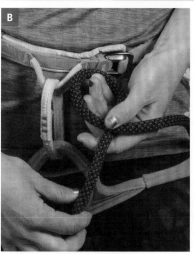

113

introductory classes and instruction. Every climbing gym has an instructional program to teach the basic skills of belaying and knot tying.

There are several different methods to tying the figure-eight retrace, but the end results are all the same. First pull out an arm's length of rope and tie an initial figure eight. Check that the tail end of the rope is about four feet long. Holding the knot to the harness and having the tail touch the ground is a good indicator of length for most adults. Feed the rope underneath the connection webbing between the leg loops and up through the waist belt where the belay loop connects. Do not position the rope against the body at the waist belt. If attached to only the connector webbing between the leg loops, the climber's center of gravity is lowered in a fall, increasing the risk of inversion. Tying in to only the waist belt creates significant force on the climber's lower back in the event of a fall.

When threading the end of the rope through the harness, keep feeding the rope through until the figure eight is mere inches from the harness, and maintain that distance while finishing the retrace process. A knot tied far away from the harness leaves a large loop that can catch on holds and pushes the entire knot system far away from the climber. Avoid twisting the strands while retracing the figure eight; keeping the knot loose makes retracing easier. Upon inspection, two parallel strands of rope create the figure-eight pattern, and a little less than a foot of rope tail is left over for the backup knot.

DRESSING AND SETTING

For knot tying, neatness counts. The finishing touch on any knot is to make sure it is neat and tight. Dressing the knot allows the climber to work out unwanted twists or adjust segment lengths of the rope. There is no excuse for a less-than-perfect knot every time you tie in. Force applied to a loose knot creates a substantial amount of rope movement. Set the knot by tightening it before use. For the figure-eight retrace, pull opposite strands of the knot to tighten it. The amount of tail left after dressing and setting the knot should be exactly six inches. No more, no less. This is the standard set by the American Alpine Club.

Though technically the climber is ready to climb after tying in, the belayer must

Opposite: To make a figure-eight follow-through: Start by threading the end of the rope up through the leg loops, following the belay loop, and then through the waist belt. The rope should be running next to (touching) the belay loop. Once you have threaded it through the harness, slide the knot toward the harness until it's a few inches away from the belay loop. Now you're ready for the more complicated part; a, Focus on keeping the end of the rope parallel to the strands that make up the figure eight; b–e, Keep the end of the rope in contact with the initial figure eight and slide it around and through the knot, f, You'll finish with both strands parallel to each other and traveling away from the climber; g, Set (pull taut) and dress (tidy all strands—no crisscrossing) this final knot, making sure it does not have gaps, h, Check that it has a tail of at least six inches.

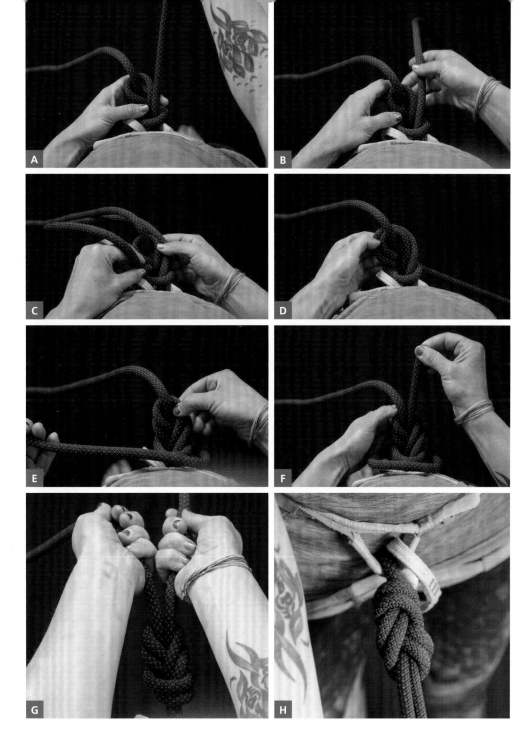

KNOT CHECKLIST

- The rope threads through the connecting webbing of the leg loops and the waist belt.
- The rewoven figure-eight knot is close to the harness.
- The pattern of the figure-eight retrace is visible and is created with untwisted parallel strands of rope.
- The knot is properly dressed and set, looking clean and compact.

also prepare for the climb. A series of checks and commands must take place to ensure both members of the party are prepared (see Climbing Commands, later in this chapter).

BELAYING

The belayer carries a significant amount of responsibility for the safety of the climbing team. While the climber concentrates on upward progress, the belayer's primary responsibilities are to maintain proper rope tension, be prepared to hold and secure the rope if the climber falls, and respond to the commands of the climber.

Without any climbing-specific gear, holding the rope of a falling climber would be difficult and unsafe. The thin diameter of the rope is too narrow for hands to hold. Even if the belayer were able to keep the rope from slipping, a heavy climber would pull a light belayer off balance or even up in the air. To help create enough friction to

securely hold the rope and fix the belayer to the ground, climbers use belay devices and anchors.

BELAYING WITH A TUBULAR BELAY DEVICE

Common belay devices are tubular, or plate-style, devices. This style of device is lightweight and cost-effective, and every climber should know how to use one properly. When the belayer works with the device, to ensure proper functionality, there is little margin of error. Knowing how to operate a tubular device is the foundation for using other devices and all belay techniques.

Getting Set Up

From the belaying end of the rope (the climber is tied in to the other end), create a "bight," or loop, of rope. Push the bight of rope through the top of the belay device, so the bight lines up with the cable of the belay device. If there are variable configurations for the belay device, start by using the one that produces the most amount of friction, referring to the device's instructions.

Attach a locking carabiner through the bight of rope and belay device cable, then clip it directly to the harness's belay loop. Get into the habit of immediately securing the locking carabiner once it is clipped and then checking the locking mechanism. Assess the lock by trying to squeeze the gate open. Visual checks are unreliable, and it is possible to mistakenly screw the gate open when trying to further close it.

When looking down at the belay device attached to your harness, the rope should travel through the device on the same side as your dominant hand. For smooth lowering, the widest end of the locking carabiner is nearest the belay device. Make sure the rope traveling up to the climber from the belay device is on top of the strand that travels to the ground.

The Brake Position

As the climber ascends, the belayer must pull slack from the rope through the belay device. When the climber needs to weight the rope, either by choice or from a fall, the belayer manually brakes the rope to keep the climber steady. For most climbers, the brake hand is the dominant hand, the one you would use to throw a ball or write. The brake hand firmly holds the brake strand directly below the belay device. This position creates a series of bends in the rope at the belay device, producing enough friction to hold the force of a climber. With the brake hand in position, the holding force is in the belay device, so the rest of the body stays relaxed.

At any moment, the belayer must be able to go into the brake position. There are several ways for a belayer to effectively carry out the task, but they all stem from the golden rule of belaying: *the brake hand must remain on the brake strand at all times!* If the climber were to fall and the belayer's brake hand were not on the brake strand, disaster would likely result. The belay technique described here allows the belayer to maintain contact between the brake strand and brake hand at all times.

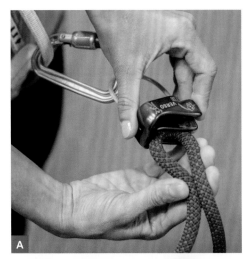

Pay close attention to loading a tubular (or any) belay device. To set it up: a, Make a bight in the rope and push it into the brake-hand side of the belay device, which is already attached to a locking carabiner on your harness belay loop; b, Pull the bight of rope through the carabiner gate, and lock the gate. Once it is set up, the rope should be loaded on the same side of the device as the belayer's brake hand. (Photos by Matt Burbach)

Taking in Slack

As the climber ascends, the rope will become loose (slack), and it is the belayer's responsibility to keep up with that slack and take it out of the top-rope system. This is an ongoing task, starting before the climber steps off the ground and ending when he returns to the ground. There are several belay methods, but they all share three principles:

1. The belayer's brake hand must remain on the brake end of the rope at all times. With the brake hand on the rope, the belayer is ready to stop a fall at any moment.

2. Hand transitions, which are the most vulnerable point in the belay sequence, should happen in the position of maximum friction to decrease the risk of losing control.

3. The belayer should take an ergonomic stance. Awkward body or hand positioning increases the risk of losing control and is biomechanically weaker than an ergonomic position.

The sequence shown—Pull, Brake, Under, Slide (PBUS)—is approved by the American Alpine Club and is quickly becoming the standard in US climbing gyms.

Starting position. Start by holding the brake strand (the end of rope coming from the belay device that does not lead to the top of the climb) about an inch away from the belay device with the brake hand. Position the brake hand so that the thumb is closer to the belay device than the pinky is. This grip is more ergonomic for braking and lowering. The guide hand (nondominant hand) grasps the climbing strand of the rope extending up to the top-rope anchor.

Pull. From the starting position, the guide hand pulls rope toward the device as the brake hand pulls rope out of the device. To allow the rope to run freely through the belay device, the brake strand of rope should run parallel to the climbing end of the rope. Pull the brake strand up to or slightly below chin height.

Brake. Once slack has been taken in, end in the brake position with the brake hand below the belay device. If the brake hand were to travel higher than eye level and the climber fell, excess slack between the brake hand and belay device would increase the distance of the climber's fall.

Under. Repositioning the hands back to the starting position is the goal of the next two phases. Take the guide hand completely off the climbing strand. Leave the brake hand in place, firmly grasping the brake strand. Move the guide hand under the brake hand, grabbing the brake strand (next to the brake hand's pinky).

Slide. Maintain contact with the rope and slide the brake hand closer to the belay device. Do not let the brake hand touch the belay device, though, because a fall at this point will pull a bit of rope through the device and potentially any part of a hand that is too close. Let go of the brake strand with the guide hand, and return the guide hand to its starting position on the climbing strand. Now the hands are in the starting position and ready to repeat the belay stroke.

If the climber ascends at a constant rate, the belayer constantly takes up slack.

In this position: a, The belayer is ready to either take in slack or brake in the event of a fall. This positon is also best when the climber is resting, or not moving, while on route. Follow these four steps to take in slack. **Pull,** b, In this phase, pull rope through the belay device with the brake hand. Pulling in rope with the guide hand will make the movement smoother. At this vulnerable point, the belayer is not in the brake position. **Brake,** c, Immediately after pulling slack through the belay device, move the hand, in one fluid motion, into the brake position. By making the brake position a part of your belay sequence, you maximize your chance of being in the brake position in the event of a fall.

Under, d, To continue the sequence, and avoid compromising the secure brake position of the brake hand, the guide hand reaches under the brake hand and grabs the brake strand. At this point, both hands are on the brake strand.

Slide, e, Relax (but don't release) your grip on the brake strand and slide the hand up the brake strand to a few inches from the belay device. The guide hand maintains slight tension on the brake strand to make sliding the brake hand up easier. From this point, you can let go with your guide hand, rest in this position, or immediately start another sequence. (Photos by Matt Burbach)

119

Because the belayer may not always see the slack in the system, especially at the climber's waist since the climber blocks the belayer's line of sight, track the movement of the climber's waist, and take in slack at the same rate. If the climber is not moving, the belayer's hands should wait in the brake position. In the case of an unexpected fall or slip, the belayer is already in the brake position and need not take any extra steps to catch the climber. As noted before, the belayer must be prepared to engage the brake position without warning.

Although learning these belay steps may seem mechanical at first, ultimately, the climber's movements and pace dictate the belayer's stroke. Proper rope tension on the climber is important. If there is too much slack, the climber may fall excessively. Too much tension can interfere with movement or even pull the climber off the wall. As belaying becomes more comfortable, learn to belay by feel. When the guide hand is extended and holding on to the climbing strand in the starting position, gently pull on the strand. This will not interfere with the climber, but when she does move up, the guide hand will drop, and then the brake hand can pull rope through the belay device.

Giving Slack

If the climber needs to reverse moves or down-climb, the belayer will need to feed out rope, or give slack. The belay stroke is simply reversed. The brake hand feeds rope into the belay device while the guide hand pulls rope out. Maintain contact between the brake hand and the brake strand, conservatively feeding out rope in small increments.

Lowering

To lower a climber, the belayer modifies the brake position to decrease the friction, and the weight of the climber pulls the rope through the belay device. The belayer must be in the brake position with the climber weighting the rope. After a fall, the climber will automatically weight the rope, but at the top of a route, the climber must let go of the wall to weight the rope before being lowered. For additional lowering security, place the guide hand above the brake hand in the brake position.

When the climber is ready to be lowered, and the climber and belayer have exchanged a series of commands (see Climbing Commands), the belayer maintains the brake position but eases the grip on the brake strand. The weight of the climber, combined with the decrease in friction, slides the rope through the belay device, lowering the climber. The belayer completely controls the climber's descent. Lower in a controlled, consistent manner, keeping the hands still. If the hands move up toward the belay device, pinching is probable and can compromise the climber's descent. Keep the brake arm straight, easing arm tension and preventing the hand from sliding up to the belay device. If lowering too quickly, the belayer can stop the climber by firmly grasping the brake strand and then restart the descent at a

Keeping the brake hand down (and brake arm straight) allows the belayer to apply maximum braking power at any point while lowering the climber. The belayer controls the rate of descent by loosening her grip and allowing the climber's weight to pull the rope through the belay device. (Photo by Matt Burbach)

slower pace. Lowering a climber should be effortless for the belayer, so keep the shoulders relaxed throughout the process. Guide the climber down until his feet are firmly on the ground and the last commands are used.

BELAYING WITH AN ASSISTED-BRAKING DEVICE

Assisted-braking belay devices have become widely used in climbing gyms. They tend to be heavier and more expensive than tubular devices, but assisted-braking devices are favored by some because they back up the belayer's brake position. The most popular model is the Petzl GriGri, which is the model you will see depicted and described in this section. Although an assisted-braking device can make belaying more comfortable (both physically and mentally), it is not foolproof and still requires attentive belaying. Because the lowering action can be different and more sensitive than a tubular device, an assisted-braking device requires practice and instruction before using with a climber. If possible, learn how to belay with a tubular device first. Learning to use an assisted-braking mechanism first can make it difficult to transition to belaying manually with a tubular device.

Getting Set Up

The instructions and the photographs in this section demonstrate the use of the Petzl GriGri, specifically. Other assisted-braking devices may work in a similar manner, but will have subtle differences specific to their design.

Pay special attention to the instructions that accompany the GriGri. To load the belay device, slide it apart along the rotating pin to expose the inside. Place the belay end of the rope inside so that the strand of rope traveling up to the climber exits the device from the climber icon on

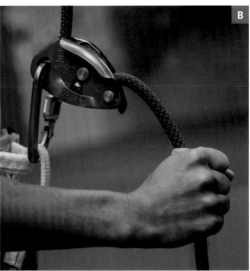

With any assisted-braking device, follow the instructions carefully. For the GriGri, make sure the brake strand of the rope matches the hand depicted on the device and the climber's end of the rope matches up with the climber icon. To set up the device for belaying: a, With the device attached to a locking carabiner clipped to the belay loop, thread rope into the device; b, Slide the moving plate closed. (Photos by Matt Burbach)

the GriGri, and the brake strand comes out from the hand illustration. Close the device and clip a locking carabiner through the open hole in the GriGri, and attach it to the belay loop on the harness, with the climber's strand nearest the body and the plastic lever pointing away from the belayer. As with any belay device, assess the setup with a preclimb check. Tug on the climber's strand of the rope traveling out of the belay device. This pull causes the self-locking mechanism to engage, as if a climber were weighting the rope. Use the proper commands to check the readiness of the climbing party (see Climbing Commands).

Taking in Slack

Taking in slack with a GriGri is identical to belaying with any other belay device: use the same PBUS sequence described for a tubular belay device. The belayer may experience more resistance pulling stiffer, thicker-diameter rope through a GriGri.

The advantages of an assisted-braking belay device are evident once the climber weights the rope and the self-locking mechanism engages. The locking mechanism inside the device pushes a lever against the rope. When locked, the brake strand requires little pressure to keep it from slipping, but keeping a secure grip provides

Steps to belaying with an assisted-braking belay device (GriGri shown here): a, Starting position; b, Pull; c, Brake; d, Under; e, Slide. (Photos by Matt Burbach)

With the GriGri, the guide hand on the lever controls the rate of descent. The farther, or harder, the belayer pulls the lever toward herself, the faster the climber will descend. Lowering a climber too slowly is rarely a problem, but belayers need to be wary of letting a descending climber pick up too much speed, as the belayer may find it hard to manage—or may even lose control of—the descent. Be cautious when lowering. Even though the guide hand controls the speed of the descent, keep the brake hand on and engaged with the brake strand.

To lower with a GriGri: a, With the weight of the climber on the rope, the belay device's assisted-braking lever is engaged, pinching the rope to prevent movement. Note the brake hand is still in the brake position, as it should be with any type of belay device. b, The left hand controls the rate of descent with the GriGri lever. Note how the brake strand runs over the curved edge of the belay device, creating a smooth rate of descent. (Photos by Matt Burbach)

backup. Even with assisted-braking devices, keep the brake hand on the brake strand at all times.

Giving Slack

The GriGri works like a seat belt: the rope can travel through the device in both directions, but when slack is pulled quickly out of the device, the locking mechanism engages. If the climber needs slack, the belayer should give it slow, short pulls to prevent the GriGri from locking. If the device locks from giving slack too quickly, stop the pull to disengage the lock, and then restart.

Lowering

If the climber weights the rope and the belayer tries lowering the climber by easing the grip on the brake strand (like with a tubular device), nothing will happen because the device is locked. It remains locked unless the climber unweights the rope or the belayer uses the device's lowering lever.

With the brake hand still holding on to the brake strand, grab the plastic lever on the device with the guide hand and rotate it up until you feel a change of tension against the lever. By pulling back farther than the initial point of tension, the pressure point on the rope opens, allowing rope to slip through the device and lower the climber. Be particularly careful lowering a climber as the lever is extremely sensitive and there is a fine line between locked and fully open, which could cause the climber to free-fall to the ground.

When lowering with a GriGri, focus on controlling the climber's descent by using the guide hand on the lever and the brake hand on the brake strand as backup. Just like with a tubular device, keep the brake arm straight, preventing the hand from creeping up into the belay device. If the climber descends too fast, let go of the lever to immediately stop the climber, but keep the brake hand secure. This may seem counterintuitive, especially after learning how to belay with a tubular device. Although a GriGri may look like an easy device to use, it requires practicing a new set of skills.

OTHER BELAY DEVICES

Climbing gear companies continue to enhance the belay device, making improvements in weight, price, functionality, and versatility. Some may offer more braking power but not feed rope out smoothly, while others may feed smoothly but come at a weight premium. While there may be slight tweaks and nuances to using devices that are different from standard tubular devices and assisted-braking devices, the overall belay technique and principles still apply.

ANCHORING

The belay system works well when the climber and belayer have a similar mass—they balance each other out. Imagine the amount of upward force that would be put on a one-hundred-pound belayer catching the fall of a climber twice his weight. To help even out weight discrepancies, gyms often wrap the top ropes around the anchors to create additional friction, but there are some other anchoring options to help manage differences in weight.

Some gyms strategically place belay anchors, or floor anchors, near the base of climbs. These pieces of nylon cord or webbing are secured to the floor and provide a direct attachment point for the belayer. This prevents belayers who are significantly lighter than their partners from being pulled off the ground. Anchors are advantageous since the belayer remains stationary, and they make for easy lowering. New belayers should consistently anchor themselves until they are able to disrupt the force of a falling climber through proper stance and body positioning.

Use an additional locking carabiner (not the one attached to the belay device) to connect the floor anchor to the belay loop below the belay device. If there are multiple attachment points on the floor anchor, attach the carabiner at the height of your belay loop. Too much slack in the anchor can pull the belayer off the ground until the anchor is pulled tight. The floor anchor must be short enough to take the force of the climber. Achieve this through a straight line between the floor anchor, belay device, and top-rope anchor.

In lieu of floor anchors, some gyms offer dynamic anchors, which is a fancy term for "a sack of something heavy." A dynamic anchor is usually a heavy, soft weight bag that the belayer can attach to himself. Because these anchors can move, they're less static than floor anchors, and the belayer may experience some upward movement as the climber moves down before the dynamic anchors activate.

The belayer's stance in relation to the anchor affects the force of a falling climber. If the belayer stands back from the anchor, a forceful fall can pull the belayer forward and to an abrupt stop by the floor anchor. Stand slightly ahead of the anchor to minimize pull from a fall. The anchor should be at the belayer's side, not between the legs. The belayer should stand with the legs slightly bent and body at a slight angle to the wall to keep the anchor running to the side.

COMMUNICATION

Many climbing accidents and incidents result from miscommunication between the climber and the belayer. Miscommunication often results from either a misunderstanding or the inability to hear a verbal command. If the climber and belayer use the same set of commands, the chance of misunderstanding decreases.

Since the climber takes on greater risk than the belayer throughout the climb, she initiates the commands, and the belayer responds verbally or with a directed action. The commands start after the party conducts their preclimb check and the climber is ready to ascend.

First, the climber says, **"On belay?"** to ask the belayer if he is ready to do his job. The belayer responds by pulling up all the slack in the top-rope system and assuming a solid belay stance. Once ready, the belayer says, **"Belay on."** From this point forward, the belayer is ready to catch the climber's fall at any point.

Once the climber is ready to step onto the wall, the last command before leaving the ground is **"Climbing,"** which lets the belayer know the climber is about to leave the ground. **"Climb on"** is the belayer's confirmation that he is aware of and ready for the climber's ascent.

As the climber ascends, she may want the belayer to perform certain tasks. For instance, she may need more or less slack while climbing or may want to weight the rope at some point. If the climber ascends quickly (or the belayer takes slack up too slowly), the climber says, **"Up rope."** The belayer then takes up slack more quickly, but not to the point of creating too much tension on the rope between the climber and belayer. If the belayer pulls too much rope in or the climber needs to step down and the rope is constricting movement,

CLIMBING COMMANDS

CLIMBER'S COMMANDS	MEANING	BELAYER'S RESPONSE	MEANING OR ACTION
"On belay?"	Ready to belay?	"Belay on"	Belay ready
"Climbing"	I am climbing	"Climb on"	Proceed climbing
"Up rope"	There is too much slack	(Action)	Take in some more rope
"Slack"	Need rope to work with	(Action)	Feed out rope
"Take"	Take my weight	"Gotcha"	Brake position
"Falling"	I am coming off	(Action)	Brake position
"Lower"	Lower me	"Lowering"	Lower the climber
"Off belay"	I am done with the belay	"Belay's off"	Verbal acknowledgment

stating **"Slack"** prompts the belayer to feed out a bit of rope.

If at any point the climber needs to weight the rope, she says, **"Take."** This tells the belayer to take up the climber's weight, and the climber can use this command at any point on the climb. In response, the belayer assumes the brake position. If the belayer is in the middle of an arm pull, taking in rope, he quickly finishes that stroke and then brakes the climber. If the belayer has been effectively taking in slack as the climber ascends, the climber will not fall far when leaning back onto the rope. There is no technical verbal response to "Take," but the belayer can say **"Gotcha."**

"Falling" is often said if the climber is in the action of falling. The climber may not have the awareness to announce a fall while midroute, though, so you should always be prepared for the brake position at any time. Once the climber has weighted the rope, eventually she will either continue to climb or be lowered. If she chooses to keep climbing, saying **"Climbing"** lets the belayer know her intentions. And if the climber is ready to lower, she can say **"Lower."** The belayer replies with **"Lowering"** and lowers the climber.

Finally, once the climber is lowered to the ground and no longer needs the assistance of a belay, she says, **"Off belay."** The belayer acknowledges with **"Belay's off"** and now can take his brake hand off the brake strand. Indoor climbers often fail to use these final commands because standing on a flat padded floor makes it fairly obvious when the climber finishes. However, these commands are essential when climbing outside, where the situation is not so obvious, so practice the full set of commands to help develop the habit. Be diligent with the exact commands. If your partner yells, "Take up the slack," and you only hear the words "take" and "slack," how will you decide what to do? Stick to the commands to limit confusion.

PUTTING THE SYSTEM TOGETHER

Redundancy is an important practice in safe climbing. Not only is equipment backed up, but the climber and belayer should practice redundancy in checking each other for proper gear setup. Distractions are frequent while putting on harnesses or tying in to the rope, so each member of the climbing party should check the other for safety. Mistakes like un-doubled-back buckles, unfinished knots, and unscrewed carabiners happen before the climber even leaves the ground, so double-checking your partner can minimize risks associated with these types of mistakes.

CONDUCTING A SAFETY CHECK

Double-check each other before every climb. Since the belayer anchors himself and is immobile, the climber may have to move to the belayer. To keep the checkup systematic, start from the body and then move outward toward the rope. When checking your climbing partner, it is a good idea to verbally inform him of what you are checking and its condition.

Checking the Belayer

Use the following list to double-check the belayer.

- **Harness.** Make sure the buckles are doubled back, harness fits securely over the hips at the waist, and webbing lies flat against the body.

- **Anchor.** If using an anchor, ensure that it is attached to the belay loop below the belay device. If not using an anchor, consider the consequences of a forceful fall. Confirm that the belayer's stance is in front of and not straddling the floor anchor.

- **Belay device.** For a tubular device, check that the locking carabiner clips through both the device's cable and the bight of rope. With an assisted-braking device, compare the brake strand and climber strand with the diagram on the device. Tug-test the climbing strand to test the locking mechanism.

- **Carabiners.** Double-check locking carabiners with a squeeze test. Do not rely on a visual check or a twist of the lock.

Checking the Climber

Use the following list to double-check the climber.

- **Harness.** Make sure the buckles are doubled back, harness fits securely over the hips at the waist, and webbing lies flat against the body.

- **Rope.** Confirm that the rope feeds through both the leg loops and waist belt.

- **Knot.** For the figure-eight retrace, see that the knot is tied, dressed, and set correctly, and that the backup knot is sufficient. Tie the primary knot and backup within a foot of the climber's harness.

Opposite: *No matter how much climbing experience you have, check yourself and your partner every time you climb.*

KEY EXERCISE: LEARNING HOW TO TOP-ROPE BELAY

When top-rope belaying, the belayer must quickly react to the climber's actions, comfortably and intuitively taking in slack and assuming the brake position. Smoothly lowering a climber is also a practiced skill.

The Goal: Learn to perform effortless belaying that feels natural and to achieve the confidence to brake a climber quickly and lower a climber smoothly, with control.

The Setup: Select a top-rope climb for this exercise. A climbing wall is not even needed, since this exercise is a practice in top-rope belaying. You can hang a rope over something high and sturdy if practicing this exercise outside of the gym.

Before belaying an actual climber, practice the belay commands, sequences, and proper rope work on the ground until you're comfortable with it all.

CONTINUED

GROUND SCHOOL TOP-ROPE BELAY EXERCISE

1. Load the belay device as if you were going to belay a climber.
2. Have your climbing partner tie in to the other strand of rope to practice tying in. There should be plenty of slack on the climber's side of the rope.
3. Go through the preclimb checklist and commands with your partner.
4. Continuously take in slack, simulating a climber's ascent. Have your partner watch your technique.
5. At various times, have the climber simulate a fall by forcibly pulling down on the rope. Go into the brake position to hold the fall.
6. Practice lowering your climber with him hanging on the rope.

CONSIDERATIONS

- Treat this exercise as if you were actually belaying. The only difference is that your partner is on the ground.
- You must be extremely proficient at this exercise before belaying a live climber.
- This exercise is still effective in practicing the belay motions without a partner and is not limited to a climbing gym.
- This exercise can also be practiced with an assisted-braking device, but do so only after developing competent use of a tubular belay device.

AUTO-BELAY SYSTEMS

In recent years, auto-belay systems, which allow for belayer-free top-roping, have grown in popularity. While some systems operate on pneumatic engineering and others use a flywheel, an auto-belay system works by creating constant upward tension on a rope or webbing. At the base of the climb, the climber clips into the system with a provided locking carabiner or two (for redundancy). As the climber ascends, the system slightly tugs upward. When the climber weights the rope or webbing, the system automatically lowers the climber to the ground. This instant lowering eliminates any chance to rest by hanging on the rope and then continuing to climb from the same spot.

The benefit of an auto-belay and the lack of a belayer is that the climber can perform laps on the wall solo. If you have a limited amount of time or don't have a partner, you can get a lot of climbing done in the gym. But for some gym operators, this does not outweigh the disadvantages. Having a partner is part of the safety protocol of top-roping—there's another person to double-check the system and go through the climbing commands. Without a partner, it's easier than you'd think to forget to double-check the system. Furthermore, climbing gyms build communities through the shared experience of members climbing with each other. By function, auto-belay systems do not contribute to that.

CLOSING THE LOOP

The relationship between climber and belayer is built on trust and competency. While the belay actions and verbal responses may feel awkward at first, practice them until they become second nature. Once you (and your climbing partner) feel confident in your skills, take your belay certification test.

As a belayer, stay focused on the task at hand. When you're belaying, you have one responsibility in life—paying attention to your climber to keep her safe. Your conversation with your buddy on the floor can wait. It's perfectly acceptable to tell him to wait until you're finished belaying to figure out postclimbing dinner plans.

ENJOYING THE VERTICAL WORLD

Top-roping is the best introduction to getting vertical. As your focus, fitness, and understanding of movement improve, you'll have so much of the gym's terrain open to you. But top-roping does have its limitation in the gym. Severely overhanging walls are generally lead climbing only, since the swing of a top rope would be too severe and potentially unsafe. If you desire to lead climb, you should first feel comfortable climbing 5.10 in the gym, on varying terrain. As described in detail in the next chapter, lead climbing introduces more technical action on the climber's part with potentially more risk, but even greater reward!

Opposite: Learning to lead climb in the gym is how many climbers progress to sport climbing outside.

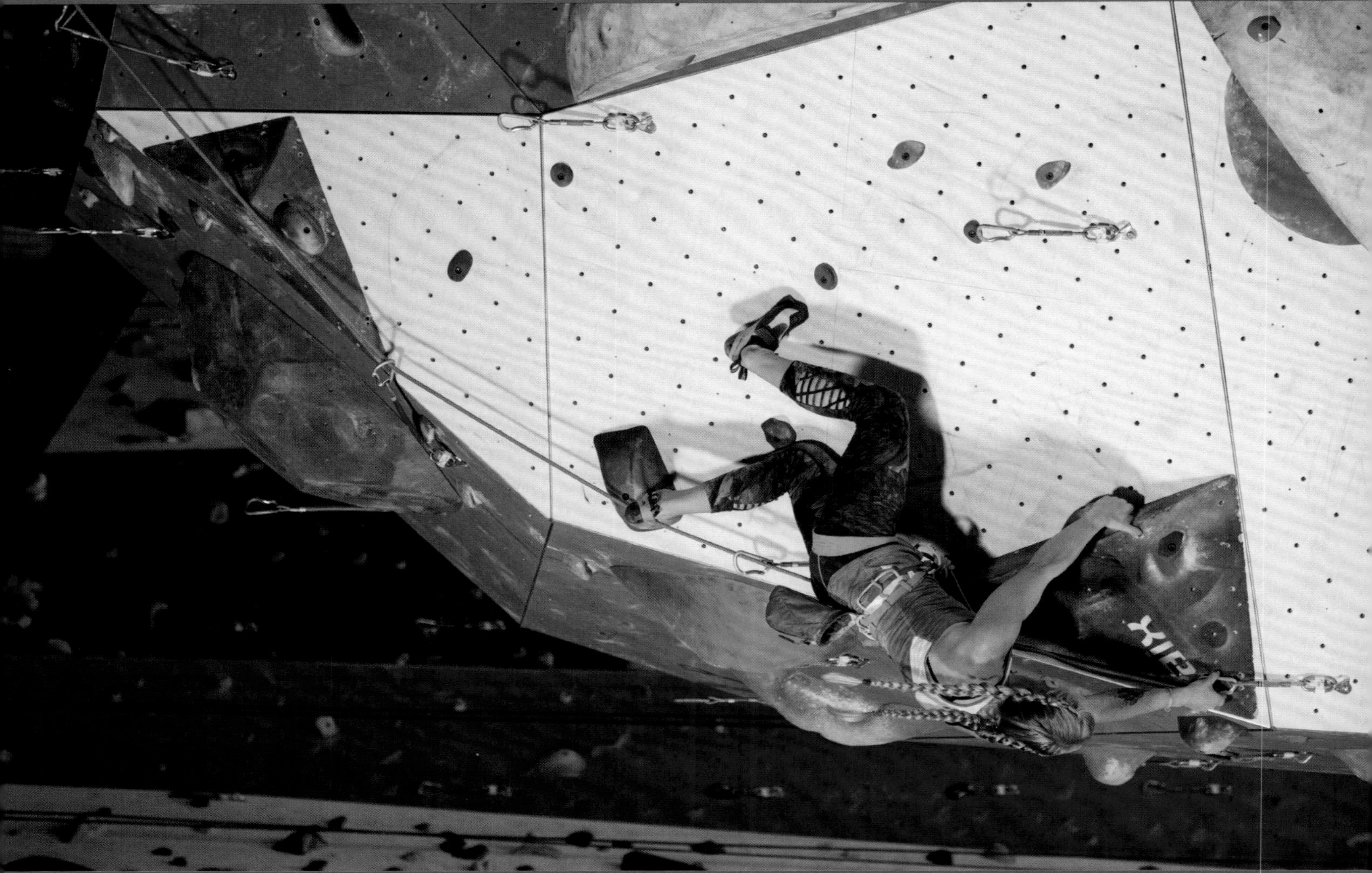

CHAPTER 6

Lead Climbing

Although top-rope climbing has many advantages—it is the easiest introduction to roped climbing, skill requirements are basic, falls are generally short and gentle, and you do not have to worry about dealing with your safety system as you climb—it also has limitations. For example, top-roping extreme overhanging or wandering routes can be unsafe, since falling can result in big swings that can endanger you or others in your path. Another limiting factor is that many climbing gyms dedicate only a portion of their total wall surface to top-rope climbing. Knowing the skills necessary only for top-roping limits your route choices if you should choose to start climbing outdoors, as the sole routes available to you will be those that can be accessed from above to set anchors.

Overcome these constraints by broadening your skill set to include lead climbing. Rather than climb on a rope already anchored at the top of the climb, lead climbers take the rope up as they climb and affix it to progressively higher anchor points along the way. In a gym environment, these anchor points generally consist of a quickdraw (two carabiners connected by a piece of nylon webbing, also known as a draw) attached to a fixed bolt. Outdoor leaders protect their climbs by placing protective gear in the rock or by clipping draws to fixed bolts.

Lead climbing allows for a freedom that top-rope climbing cannot provide. Once you are a proficient leader, your choice of gym routes will be limited only by your skill. You will be able to explore new terrain, such as meandering routes or those that go through large overhangs. Because lead climbing involves setting anchor points in addition to moving up the wall, it is more mentally engaging than top-rope climbing.

Lead climbing has its own constraints and considerations, however. For example, instead of worrying about big top-rope swings, you must be prepared for longer falls than in top-roping—a leader who falls from a point above the last clipped bolt travels the distance to that bolt and then that distance again. These longer falls end with a sudden jerk as the rope pulls taut.

Leading also requires greater endurance, poise, and efficiency than top-roping the same grade, since you must stop several times during a lead route to pull up slack with one hand and clip the rope into the quickdraw.

GETTING STARTED

Both lead climbing and lead belaying require even greater focus and care than top-rope climbing and belaying. Decisions must be made quickly as the belayer reacts to the climber and vice versa. Many climbers enter the world of leading through learning to be a competent lead belayer, and, in fact, this an excellent way to familiarize yourself with the rhythm, flow, and technique involved in leading. Conversely, learning to lead climb will make you a better lead belayer, as you will develop a keener understanding of the need for efficiency throughout the whole operation. Although you will most likely lead belay before you ever lead climb, begin with the mechanics of lead climbing first, as it is the "action" in the action-reaction system of lead belaying.

LEAD CLIMBING GEAR

For liability reasons and to monitor the number of lead climbers at a given time, some climbing gyms provide lead ropes. A gym's lead ropes are thicker, more durable,

Lead climbing allows you to climb the steepest, most daunting features of the gym, like arches and overhanging roofs.

and shorter than personal climbing ropes. To verify lead climbing and belaying competency, many gyms require that you check out a rope from the staff. Other gyms may leave ropes available on the floor. Check with your gym for their policy, as well as a minimum length requirement.

Fixed carabiners attached to bolts are the industry standard for protection. Steel carabiners or chain links instead of webbing make these quickdraws more durable. The gates of these draws are heavier than a standard aluminum gate but work just the same. For the climber's safety, do not grab the carabiner as a hold for clipping, even in desperation or to make a clip. Nylon webbing or steel cable, when covered, is difficult to hold, and grabbing the carabiner does not allow any room to attach the rope and increases the risk for hand or finger injury.

RESPONSIBILITIES OF A LEAD CLIMBER

Because the commitment level of lead climbing is greater than top-roping, it is not something beginners should jump right into. Those attempting to learn how to lead climb should feel confident climbing a grade of at least 5.10 on a top rope. While this is not a magic grade, gyms seldom set lead routes easier than 5.9. And even more important than the ability to ascend a certain grade is a solid foundation in movement and kinesthetic awareness. If your climbing is not yet smooth and graceful, consider putting in more time on

your technique before embarking on lead climbing. Remember, as a lead climber, you contend with not only the actual act of climbing but also managing and clipping the rope to ensure your safety.

In leading, decisions you make can affect your own safety as well as that of your belayer. To stack the odds in your favor, practice all of the skills necessary to promote safe climbing. Even before mock leading (i.e., leading while on top rope), carefully review and practice all of the following exercises and skills.

SELECTING YOUR ROUTE AND PREPPING YOUR GEAR

Before tying in to the sharp end of the rope (the lead climber's end of the rope) to begin leading, consider your route and its surrounding environment. Having a real assessment of your own climbing ability will prevent you from taking on routes that are too challenging. If your climbing limit is 5.9 on less-than-vertical routes with crimps, you should think twice about getting on a long, steep 5.9 with big moves between jugs.

Also consider the safety of the surrounding environment before getting on a climb. Check to see if other leaders may cross your route or vice versa. If so, wait until they are finished, or climb another route. Keep an eye out for miscellaneous gear left at the base of a route, and move it if there is any chance of it getting in your team's way. Think about wearing a helmet while lead climbing. The added safety provided by a helmet will give you an

REFRESHER: CONDUCTING A SAFETY CHECK

This is an abbreviated version of the checklist provided in Chapter 5, Top-Rope Climbing.

CHECKING THE BELAYER

Both members of the team should double-check the belayer for these items.

- **Harness** is on properly with buckles doubled back or otherwise secured as dictated by the style of harness.
- **Anchor** is properly affixed to belayer, if required.
- **Belay device** is properly loaded.
- **Carabiners** are locked.
- **Rope** is properly flaked on the floor and is free of kinks.

CHECKING THE CLIMBER

Both members of the team should double-check the climber for these items.

- **Harness** is on properly with buckles doubled back or otherwise secured as dictated by style of the harness.
- **Rope** passes through necessary points on harness.
- **Knot** is tied correctly.

---

increased sense of security, which is comforting, especially for the beginning leader.

TYING IN AND CHECKING OUT

To tie in to the rope, grab the rope end that sits on top of the stack and affix it to your harness using either a figure-eight follow-through knot or a bowline. Some climbers prefer tying in with the bowline because it is easier to untie after the stress of a lead fall, but if you are not comfortable with tying this knot, a figure eight will work fine (see Tying In, in Chapter 5).

With your belayer, go through the same safety check as you would if you were climbing on a top-rope system to make sure that the system is closed and that each of you have set up your equipment properly. Remember, an easy way to perform a thorough check of the system is to start your check with those elements that are closest to your body, such as your harness and knot, and then follow the rope through the system, ending with the harness of your belayer. Along the way, you will verify that your belayer has set up the belay device properly and that the rope has been flaked (stacked) to avoid tangling.

COMMUNICATION

An open line of communication is imperative between the climber and belayer,

REFRESHER: CLIMBING COMMANDS

CLIMBER'S COMMANDS	MEANING	BELAYER'S RESPONSE	MEANING OR ACTION
"On belay?"	Ready to belay?	"Belay on"	Belay ready
"Climbing"	I am climbing	"Climb on"	Proceed climbing
"Clipping"	I am pulling up rope to clip	(Action)	Feed out rope to clip
"Slack"	Need rope to work with	(Action)	Feed out rope
"Take"	Take my weight	"Gotcha"	Brake position
"Falling"	I am coming off	(Action)	Brake position
"Lower"	Lower me	"Lowering"	Lower the climber
"Off belay"	I am done with the belay	"Belay's off"	Verbal acknowledgment

especially indoors with multiple climbing parties in close proximity. The commands for lead climbing are similar to top-rope climbing. In lead climbing, the commands "On belay?" and "Belay on" signify that the belayer is ready, but it should be noted that the leader is not truly protected by the belayer until the first draw is clipped. The command chain presented in Chapter 5, Top-Rope Climbing, follows from there, but some leaders use "Clipping" to let the belayer know that slack is needed to clip the next bolt. If your belayer can see you and is paying attention, however, this call should not be necessary.

BEFORE THE FIRST CLIP

Once safety and commands have been established, the climber can start up the wall. Keep in mind, though, that a fall before making the first clip will result in hitting the ground. There are a couple of precautions you and your belayer may want to take to prepare.

If the opening moves of the climb are difficult, preclipping the first bolt is not a bad idea—staying safe should be your first priority. If possible, climb up an easier neighboring route, properly clip the rope into the first quickdraw, and climb back down to the ground. Make sure to confirm the role of the belayer before you attempt this maneuver because you may choose to down-climb or be lowered from the first bolt.

Another option for protecting a fall prior to the first bolt is to have the belayer spot the climber during the opening moves of the route. With this approach, your belayer will first pay out enough slack for you to clip the first draw and then assume a spotting position as in bouldering (see Chapter 4, Bouldering). As soon as you have clipped the first bolt, the belayer takes in the appropriate amount of slack, and you will be on belay.

CLIPPING THE ROPE CORRECTLY

The correct way to clip a rope into a carabiner is with the climbing end running

Since the rope is ineffective until it is attached to the wall, the belayer should spot the climber, just like in bouldering, until the first quickdraw is clipped.

up along the wall and then out through the carabiner to the climber. An incorrectly clipped rope, also known as a back-clipped rope, passes through the carabiner from the climbing side and then into the wall. Because a back-clipped rope can become unclipped in the event of a fall, great care should be taken to ensure that you clip the rope correctly every single time.

Correct clip: *The rope runs from the ground, up the wall, and then out from a correctly clipped quickdraw. In the event of a fall, the rope will pull taut without twisting the draw.*

CORRECT

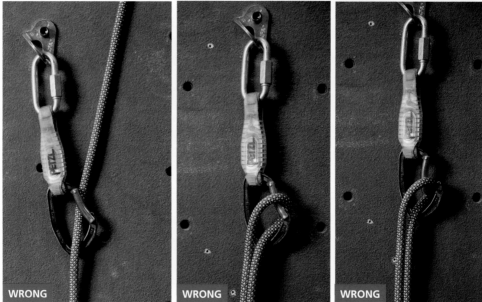

WRONG WRONG WRONG

Incorrect clips: *Because the rope runs from the clipped draw into the wall, the rope could run over the gate of this incorrectly clipped quickdraw during a fall, causing it to unclip unintentionally, as shown here.*

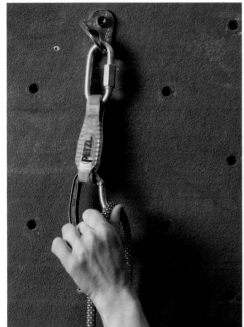

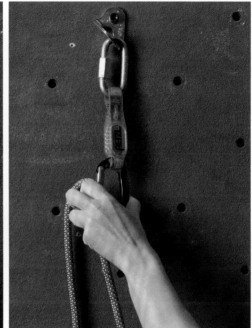

With the gate facing the opposite direction (right) of the hand she's clipping with (left), Emily uses the middle-finger grab technique.

Clipping quickdraws efficiently requires practice, particularly when pinching the draw to clip the rope, as Emily demonstrates here.

Clipping the Rope to the Quickdraw

The mechanics of clipping the rope into a quickdraw are as simple as they seem; however, applying those mechanics with pumped-out forearms and shaking legs can make things much more complicated. The use of a practiced, fluid, efficient technique is an absolute necessity.

The following section introduces methods for efficient clipping. Although these are not the only ways you might get the rope into the carabiner, they are among the most commonly used. If these styles do not work well for you, experiment with other approaches. Ultimately, the best way is the fastest and most comfortable option for you. When encountering a quickdraw, the gate will either face toward or away from you, and this determines how you grab and handle the rope before clipping.

Middle-finger grab technique. Use this method when clipping a carabiner whose gate faces the opposite direction as the hand you are clipping with, such as when the gate faces right and you are clipping with your left hand. Stabilizing the quickdraw with

141

the middle finger makes clipping easy. If the carabiner is positioned against the wall on less-than-vertical or vertical terrain, the middle finger can pull the draw away from the wall for trouble-free clipping.

Pinch technique. Use this technique when the carabiner gate is on the same side of the quickdraw as your clipping hand, such as when the gate is facing to the left and you are clipping with your left hand. Most people find this way of clipping more challenging than stabilizing the draw with the middle finger. Practicing both techniques on a carabiner hanging close to the ground will help you to improve rapidly.

UNCLIPPING

When you clip the wrong quickdraw or back-clip a carabiner, unclipping the rope tends to be more difficult than clipping it. Regardless of which side the carabiner gate faces, grab the entire carabiner and push the gate open with a free finger or thumb. With the gate open, turn the carabiner upside down to allow gravity to slide the rope out. Let go of the carabiner and make the correct clip. Undoubtedly, the rope will catch on the key-lock groove of the open carabiner; some creative wiggling will help slide the rope free.

THE DREADED Z CLIP

One of the benefits of indoor leading is that the bolts are often spaced closer together than you would find on an outdoor route. This limits the length of falls and provides an added sense of security. One drawback, though, is the tendency to Z clip.

A proper clip: the climber has grabbed the rope between her harness and the last quickdraw.

A BAD   B BAD

An improper clip creates so much friction that the climber will be unable to keep moving up. In this scenario, a, The climber grabs the rope below the quickdraw she just clipped; b, Then she moves to clip. As she moves up to the next clip, the rope is in a Z formation. It travels up, then down, and then back up the wall.

The Z clip is formed when a lead climber grabs the rope from below an already clipped quickdraw. This results in the rope traveling from the belayer to the highest clipped draw, back down to the lower draw, and then back up to the climber. When this happens, the rope drag is so great that the climber is prevented from moving up. Z clipping also effectively removes the higher bolt from the system, leaving the lower bolt as the highest anchor point. This creates the potential for longer falls, which are always less desirable.

To avoid Z clipping, grab the rope directly below the tie-in point at the harness, not farther down the rope. This ensures that the end of the rope that you clip in to the next draw is attached to you and is not the middle section below the last draw. If a Z clip does occur, simply unclip the higher carabiner and then properly reclip.

BODY POSITIONING

Because clipping requires the climber to momentarily let go with one hand, body positioning should allow for the most stable and restful stance. The body should be relaxed, with the skeletal system and legs taking the weight of the climber. Feet should be still and secure, and the quick-draw should be within reach.

The optimal body position for clipping a draw is with the carabiner at chest or stomach height. If you move much higher above the carabiner before you clip, you may find yourself forgetting to clip or moving too far past the bolt. If the carabiner is too high above you, you will be forced to take out an excess amount of rope to clip, which not only requires more effort but also creates potential for a longer fall.

Imagine, for a moment, that you are clipping a draw that is a foot above your waist and your waist is ten feet above your last clipped bolt. In this case, eleven feet of rope would be needed to clip your bolt. Now imagine that you are clipping that same bolt from a lower stance so that the bolt is about four feet above your waist, requiring you to reach over your head to clip. You would need to pull enough slack into the system to give you the eleven feet of rope required to span the distance between the two bolts, plus the additional four feet required for the rope to come back down from the bolt to your waist. In the first case, if you fell while clipping, you would take a slightly longer than twenty-two-foot fall. In the second case, your fall would be a little more than thirty feet. Which would you prefer?

Also consider that rope drag and friction between the rope and the previously clipped carabiner alters clipping. If several draws are already clipped, or the route changes directions or angles, the drag can be heavy enough to make hauling up enough rope in one pull very difficult. In this case, pull up enough rope to reach your mouth, and gently hold it in your teeth. Quickly grab another pull of rope and immediately release the bit between your teeth. Take care with this practice, as you can imagine the repercussions of falling while biting down on the climbing rope.

If you are uncertain that the quick-draw is close enough to clip, reach out and attempt to touch it. Try not to contact the carabiner too hard, though, because a swinging draw is hard to clip. Once you are ready to clip, make the commitment and follow through. As mentioned earlier, you may want to inform your belayer of your intent by saying "Clipping!" As you pull rope out to clip, keep your entire body still as you execute the move. Any excess movement can throw you off balance or cause an unexpected slip. Keep your eye on the draw until the rope is secured and the gate closed. Rush the process, and you may bobble the clip and have to try again.

Matt's body is relaxed and positioned over his feet with his left arm straight. This balance makes letting go and clipping with his right hand more comfortable.

KEY EXERCISE: LEARNING HOW TO EFFICIENTLY CLIP AND UNCLIP QUICKDRAWS

A lead climber must be able to quickly and safely clip the climbing rope into fixed quickdraws. The more time spent with the rope pulled out to clip, the more potential there is for falling. Often, strenuous body positioning, rope drag, or an awkwardly placed draw adds difficulty to the task. Unclipping is equally important. Back-clipping or clipping the wrong draw requires unclipping to correct the problem. This skill is essential when following a lead climb.

The Goal: Master a quick, efficient clip and unclip, performed with either hand and with the quickdraw gate facing either left or right.

The Setup: Position the quickdraw at eye level on the climbing wall. There should be enough hand- and footholds for the climber to stay on the wall and vary body positioning.

CLIPPING AND UNCLIPPING EXERCISE

1. Tie in to the rope as if you were lead climbing. Closely flake the rope near the wall.
2. Comfortably position yourself on the wall, just off the ground and within reach of the draw. Although the holds and terrain will dictate your exact body positioning, focus on keeping your weight over your feet and relaxing as much as possible.

Gain proficiency by clipping near the ground when the consequences are less severe; use both hands in multiple clipping stances and positions before attempting to lead a route.

3. Clip the rope into the carabiner, focusing on efficiency and quickness.
4. Unclip the rope from the carabiner, and repeat the exercise until you can quickly and comfortably clip and unclip with either hand and with either gate orientation.

CONSIDERATIONS

- To practice multiple scenarios, turn the carabiner gate in both directions to use both styles of clipping.
- Use creative clipping stances. Roofs can require clipping behind your head, and you may need to cross your arm in front of your body. The more variations practiced, the better prepared you are on a climb.
- Practicing clips from different types of holds will foster confidence. Underclings require different body positioning than slopers.
- Because the rope is not running through any draws before clipping there will not be any rope drag. To prepare for potential rope drag, use the "bite" technique in the exercise when clipping draws above the chest. By reaching for the second pull of rope while biting the first pull in your teeth, the rope drag will be less than on an actual climb.

THE GROUND FALL ZONE

Just because you have clipped the first bolt does not necessarily mean you are safe from a ground fall, even with an attentive belayer. In fact, the most potentially dangerous area for a leader is between clipping the first and second draws. A fall in this "ground fall zone" can be injurious to both the climber and belayer.

By way of demonstration, assume a quickdraw is established every ten feet on a route, and you are in position to clip the second bolt, but you have not yet pulled up the rope. Your waist might be about two feet below the draw, eight feet above the first draw, and eighteen feet above the ground. If you were to fall at that point, you would travel a minimum of sixteen feet toward the ground (twice the distance from the last draw clipped). Slack in the rope, stretch in the system, and a fall with enough force to pull the belayer forward even a little would result in a ground fall. A ground fall would be even more likely if you were in the process of pulling rope up to clip the second bolt, as you'd have that much more rope out between you and your belayer.

Many gyms try to design their lead routes so that the first and second bolts are close to each other. However, since you are responsible for your own safety, keep in mind the real risks and dangers in the ground fall zone.

ROPE MANAGEMENT

Proper rope management can help protect you if you do fall. When lead climbing, the rope either travels above you to your

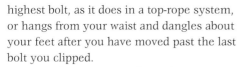

With the rope running down from the climber and against the wall, the climber's legs are free to move away from the wall in a fall.

If the rope runs over the climber's leg, a fall could either flip the climber upside down or cause a rope burn on her leg. Avoid letting the rope run over the outside of the legs or body.

highest bolt, as it does in a top-rope system, or hangs from your waist and dangles about your feet after you have moved past the last bolt you clipped.

As a rule, you want to keep the rope between your body and the wall. The rope can hang between your legs or off to one side or the other. The route the rope travels below you will help determine where exactly you want the rope to run in relationship to your body. At all times, avoid having the rope pass behind one or both of your legs and then down to your highest anchor point. This hazard, known as back-stepping

the rope, puts the climber in potential danger for an inverted fall.

If the climber back-steps the rope during a fall, the rope pulls tight around the legs, but the upper body continues to fall, causing a headfirst fall. This is extremely dangerous because the back and head will most likely be the first parts of the body to hit the wall. To avoid back-stepping the rope, pay close attention to the line your rope takes below you and take great care to dance around it in whatever way necessary to prevent it from dragging behind your legs.

FALLING

Knowing how to take a fall is a part of lead climbing. A difficult move, spinning holds, or an unexpected slip can send a climber airborne. Although falls are often over before you know it, there may occasionally be enough time in flight to prepare for impact.

As soon as you feel that you are falling, gently push out with your hands and feet to ensure that your body clears the wall. This is particularly important on vertical or less-than-vertical terrain. Falling too close to the wall can result in your face or knees scraping the climbing surface. Note that when using this technique, you do not want to push off too hard, as pushing off with too much force will slam you into the wall as the rope tightens at the end of the fall.

While falling, do not grab the draws; if you must grab the rope, grab it as close to you as possible. You can injure (or even lose) fingers by holding on to a fixed-draw carabiner while falling. Rope-burned hands can result from holding on to the rope as it pulls taut.

Falling with a stiff body is the sure way to sustain an impact injury. At the end of the fall, feet and hands should be shoulder-width apart with the knees slightly bent. This may require bringing your feet up to cushion your body and absorb the force and prevent your knees from hitting the wall. Leaning forward during the fall can cause

As he falls, Matt is relaxed and looking for his impact zone. His fall will be relatively soft because of his body positioning and the steepness of the route.

Because this route travels from right to left near the anchors, a, Clipping the anchors in the same direction creates smooth rope angles and, b, Minimizes impact on the hardware and rope for the descent.

your torso and arms to slam into the wall before your feet, so be careful. Keep your eyes open and try to watch the wall as you are falling. When the rope is pulled tight and you swing into the wall, look for a spot that your feet can hit that is clear of holds.

The fear of falling stems from the fear of the unknown. Taking short practice falls can help alleviate the anxiety of falling.

LEAD ANCHORS

The last pieces of fixed protection on an indoor lead route should consist of two anchors to provide redundancy, which is an integral characteristic of any climbing anchor. The system used varies, depending on the climbing facility. In some cases, the anchors may be two draws with the gates facing in opposite directions. Clip the rope into both carabiners so that the gates are in opposition. Another popular option is a spring-loaded anchor, a hooked piece of metal with a spring-loaded gate similar to a carabiner gate at the top. With these anchors, lay the rope on the gates from the top, and the rope will snap into place. To prevent excessive rope wear, clip the rope into the anchors in the same direction as the climb finishes. For example, if the route finishes by moving from left to right, clip the rope in to the anchors so that the climber is lowered on the right side.

RESPONSIBILITIES OF A LEAD BELAYER

Belaying a leader is much more involved than belaying a top-rope climber. The lead belayer must constantly adapt to meet the movements and needs of the climber—providing slack as the climber is clipping or moving above her last anchor point and taking rope in as the climber moves toward a clipped bolt. Absolute focus from the belayer and an open line of communication are imperative for ensuring safety.

ANCHORING THE BELAYER

The choice to use an anchor while belaying a lead climber is the subject of ongoing debate. Although there are pros and cons to anchoring, ultimately, the belayer must decide which method works best for him. Belayers should be comfortable with both methods, anchored and unanchored, as some climbing gyms do have such strong preferences that they require the use of only one method.

Choosing to Use an Anchor

Lead falls generate a significant amount of force on the belayer. An attentive belayer can brake any fall, but absorbing the force of the fall can be problematic. When a lead climber falls, the force may be enough to even lift you off your feet, especially if you weigh significantly less than the climber or if there is a substantial amount of slack in the system. If you are pulled off your feet, you will likely swing into the wall, potentially compromising your ability to maintain the brake position. In extreme cases, the belayer can even be pulled up to and stopped by the first bolt. The more travel the belayer experiences, the farther the climber falls.

Proper anchoring will allow you to remain stationary upon feeling the impact of the climber's fall. Anchoring reduces the dynamic nature of the belay system, though, and can impair your ability to soften the fall of the climber. But some of the force of the fall will be absorbed by stretch and slight slippage of the rope, tightening of the knot, and the little bit that you are pulled forward even though you are anchored.

Climbing gyms most often make floor anchors out of webbing or static line that is attached to permanent fixtures in the floor. Usually these anchors will have various clip-in points along their length. Clip in to the point that provides for a tight anchor but not so tight that your harness is pulled uncomfortably toward the floor. Clip the floor anchor to your belay loop using a separate carabiner from the one that is clipped to your belay device. Be sure to clip the anchor carabiner to your belay loop at a point below the belay carabiner.

Once you are anchored, orient your body so that your chest is facing in the direction of the first bolt. Rather than stand with your feet side by side, place one leg (the one opposite your belay hand) farther forward, and slightly bend both knees. This position will help you to plant your weight into your back leg to resist being yanked forward even the short distance the anchor may allow.

Ultimately, with proper body positioning and stance, the belay system (with you in the middle) will form a straight line from the anchor point on the ground up to the first bolt. If you have not already achieved this stance, the force of the climber's fall will create this line for you, snapping you into place in a violent pull.

After your climber has reached the ground and you have taken her off belay, do not assume all potential for accidents has passed. As comical as it may sound, you can take a pretty embarrassing fall by trying to walk away while still anchored; so do not forget to unclip!

Choosing Not to Anchor to the Floor

Some argue that there are more advantages to belaying unanchored than to belaying anchored. When you are not anchored to one spot on the floor, you have the freedom to find the safest belay stance as the climber moves. For example, you may position yourself to the right of the climber and against the wall until the first bolt is clipped and then move to the other side of the climber at a later time. If slack must be taken in quickly, you can take it up simply by stepping back from the wall. Also, the "give" of an unanchored belayer at the point of impact from a climber's fall adds to the dynamic nature of the belay and allows the belayer to help soften the climber's fall.

If you are new to lead belaying, you may prefer to anchor to have the added comfort of knowing you are grounded. However, if you weigh about the same as your climber, the benefits of anchored belaying are diminished, particularly if you use a strong stance to firmly ground yourself.

Belayer positioning. The position of the belayer affects the safety of the climber. Stand too far away from the wall, and the climber can fall directly onto the span of rope that stretches between you and the first clipped bolt. In contrast, the climber can fall on top of you if you are positioned directly against the wall and under the climber. To consider the best spot from which to belay, ask yourself:

- Where does the route start and travel?
- Where is the first bolt?
- What hand will the climber clip with first, and where will his stance be at the first bolt?

By answering these questions, bearing in mind your goal of keeping the rope out of the climber's way, you can find the best position from which to belay. Generally, you want to stand relatively close to the wall, off to one side of the first bolt, and not underneath your climber. This will allow you to keep the rope out from under the climber's feet. Once the climber ascends higher than the third or fourth bolt on the route, you can move back from the wall to enable you to see the climber's movements and anticipate his needs.

PRECLIMB ROPE MANAGEMENT

After choosing a belay position and whether or not to anchor, uncoil and neatly stack the rope by simply running its length through your hands and letting it form a small pile on the floor at your feet. Be sure to keep track of the end of the rope that is at the top of the stack, as this is the end that the climber will tie in to. Stacking

GOOD

BAD

Good belay stance: *Here, the belayer stands close enough to the wall to minimize outward force and the rope angle on the first draw, but far enough way so that the climber won't land on him in the event of a low fall.* **Bad belay stance:** *This belayer is positioned way too far from the wall. A fall will pull the belayer forward rather than up, and the larger amount of rope out increases the odds of the climber hitting the ground.*

the rope will help you to smoothly feed rope to your climber and minimizes the potential for the rope to form tangles as it is paid out.

BELAY MOTION

The principles of belaying a leader are the same as in top-rope belaying, except that you must provide slack to your climber in addition to taking up rope as she climbs. If you are accustomed to belaying top-rope climbers only, providing slack may feel a bit counterintuitive and will require some practice.

As discussed in Chapter 2, Equipment, there are many different styles of belay devices, and the type of belay device will dictate the techniques you use for paying out and taking in slack and for lowering. Tubular belay devices are often used for their ease of use, low cost, and light weight. However, the indoor and sport climbing communities have also embraced assisted-braking belay devices, such as the Petzl

GriGri, even though these tend to be much heavier and more costly and require a substantial amount of practice to ensure efficient and safe use.

Belaying with a Tubular Belay Device

The basic techniques for using a tubular belay device to belay a lead climber are similar to the techniques discussed in Chapter 5, Top-Rope Climbing. The primary difference is the practice of providing slack to the lead climber.

Paying out slack. As the climber moves away from his last clipped bolt or needs some slack to clip a carabiner, the belayer must feed rope to the climber (also known as giving rope or slack). The climber's speed and the length of rope required to clip a bolt will dictate the amount of rope given by the belayer.

To feed out slack, hold the climbing side of the rope with the guide hand near the belay device and with the thumb up. The brake hand should grasp the brake strand of the climbing rope comfortably away from the body. Though the more ergonomic position for the brake hand is palm down, most belayers find a palm-up position to be more comfortable. As the climber needs more rope from the belayer, push rope into the belay device with the brake hand while simultaneously pulling rope through with the guide hand. The finishing position for one stroke of arm movement is with the brake hand near the belay device (but not touching it) and the guide hand extended away from the body. To reposition the hand back into the start of the sequence, hold the brake hand still while sliding the guide hand toward the belay device. As soon as the guide hand has control of the rope and is still, slide the brake hand away from the belay device to the start position. From here, repeat the sequence with the appropriate frequency and speed to keep your climber safe. Short, choppy pulls of rope to the climber can be avoided by paying out a full arm's length of rope as needed. As with top-rope climbing, maintain control of the brake strand with the brake hand at all times.

As the climber pulls out rope to make a clip, he may have to make more than one pull to reach the quickdraw. In this case, the belayer should try to match the amount of rope pulled up by the climber. The climber requires special attention from the belayer while clipping, because a fall with all that rope pulled up to clip can be disastrous. If the climber were to fall with rope out to clip, the belayer can quickly take in slack. As soon as the climber clips the rope into the draw, the belayer should take in the slack to maintain the proper rope tension.

Taking up rope. As a climber moves up toward a clipped bolt or as he down-climbs from an unclipped bolt, the belayer must take in the slack that is created. Failure to do so may leave excess slack in the system, which could result in an exceptionally long fall. The motion that is used to take up rope is identical to top-rope belaying (see Chapter 5).

Braking a fall. The major difference between braking a lead fall and a top-rope fall is that lead falls often generate significantly

When lead belaying with a tubular device: a, Keep the brake hand on the brake strand at all times, just as in top-rope belaying; b, Feed out slack as the climber moves up the wall or is clipping, pulling slack out of the belay device with the guide hand as the brake hand pushes rope into the device. The belayer can move toward or away from the first clip to adjust the amount of slack as well.

more force than top-rope falls, as the climber is often falling a greater distance. For this reason, the belayer must be ready at any time, even though a climber may use the command "Falling" to warn his belayer to anticipate the impact. Although the climbing may be easy and the leader may feel comfortable, spinning holds and unexpected slips can catch the team off guard.

Lowering. By clipping the rope into the anchors at the top of a lead climb, the climber establishes a standard slingshot top-rope system. Even if the climber is not at the anchors, he can still be lowered to the ground at any point. To bring the climber down, use the same lowering techniques as in top-rope climbing (see Chapter 5).

Belaying with an Assisted-Braking Belay Device

The greatest benefit of an assisted-braking belay device is its ability to lock the rope during a fall, thus aiding the belayer in braking the system. The device's locking mechanism is similar to that of a car seat belt. If rope is pulled out in a smooth, slow manner, it will slide easily. However, pulling the rope through the device too quickly or with too strong of a pull will lock up the device. The device is unlocked with the release of a lever. In most other ways, using an assisted-braking device is similar to using a tubular device.

As in Chapter 5, the instructions and the photographs in this section are specific to the Petzl GriGri, a popular assisted-braking belay device. Most assisted-braking devices work in a similar manner, though there may be subtle variations among the different designs.

Paying out slack. When the climber moves up the wall at a slow or constant rate, feeding rope is the same as with a tubular device. To quickly feed rope to a climber, the belayer must hold the locking mechanism in a disengaged position. To do this, start with the brake hand holding the brake strand right next to the belay device with the palm facing up. For the belayer who brakes with the right hand, position the brake hand's thumb against the brake lever to prevent the brake-lever arm from locking. Be sure the brake hand maintains control of the brake strand while pushing the brake lever against the body of the device with the bottom of the hand. With the brake lever disengaged, the guide hand can smoothly pull rope to give slack to the climber. Be extremely cautious while pushing the brake lever against the belay device, and do so only while feeding rope. If slack needs to be taken up quickly, the brake hand must be able to pull rope through the device immediately.

Taking up rope. There is no difference in taking in slack with an assisted-braking device compared to a tubular belay device. Because of the increased friction of the rope running through the device, inefficient technique can make taking in rope more difficult. Remember to pull rope toward the belay device with the guide hand while simultaneously pulling rope away from the device with the brake hand.

Braking a fall. The brake position and act of braking a fall is the same with an assisted-braking device as it is with a tubular device, although, with the braking mechanism, the force and effort needed by the brake hand to hold a fall is minimal. This does not mean, however, that you should disregard the importance of the brake hand when using an assisted-braking device. You must still keep your brake hand on the brake strand of the rope at all times.

Lowering. Lowering a lead climber with a device like the GriGri is the same as with a top-rope climber. With the brake hand still holding on to the brake strand, grab the plastic lever on the device with the guide hand, and rotate it up until you feel a change of tension against the lever. By pulling back farther than the initial point of tension, the pressure point on the

The assisted-braking mechanism in the GriGri prevents the belayer from quickly pulling out slack: a, In this case, from the belay device with the guide hand. To disengage the assisted-braking mechanism: b, Push down on the lever with the thumb of the brake hand to keep the rope running smoothly through the device. Even through this movement, the brake hand always maintains control of the brake strand, allowing the belayer to go into the brake position at any time; c, The belayer disengages the assisted-braking mechanism to allow her to give the climber slack quickly.

KEY EXERCISE: LEARNING HOW TO LEAD BELAY

Keeping a lead climber safe requires not only vigilant attention on the belayer's part, but also quick reflexes. The lead belayer constantly adjusts to the climber's movements and ultimately prevents a ground fall while minimizing the climber's flight time.

The Goal: Learn to improve reaction time when feeding out rope, taking in slack, and assuming the brake position without belaying an active climber.

The Setup: In an area with ample floor space, flake the climbing rope and load the belay device. Your partner ties into the climbing end of the rope, facing away from you.

To learn how to transition seamlessly between taking in rope and feeding out slack as a lead belayer, practice on the ground until switching back and forth becomes natural.

GROUND SCHOOL LEAD BELAY EXERCISE

1. With your climbing partner, double-check the setup and go through the commands as if climbing a vertical route.
2. Instead of climbing up a wall, the climber walks away from the belayer, simulating an ascent.
3. The belayer feeds out rope appropriate to the walking speed of the climber.
4. The climber should periodically stop and simulate clipping a quickdraw or down-climbing by walking back toward the belayer. The belayer should react accordingly.
5. At some point, have the climber run forward to simulate a fall.

CONSIDERATIONS

- You can perform this exercise with either a tubular device or assisted-braking device.
- Practice feeding enough rope so that the climber's forward movement is not limited, but not so much rope that it sags on the ground.
- Without a floor anchor, pay special attention to stance. If not, you will be pulled off your feet.

rope opens, allowing rope to slip through the device and lower the climber. Focus on controlling the climber's descent by using the guide hand on the lever, with the brake hand backing up the descent from the brake strand. Just like with a tubular device, keep the brake arm straight, preventing the hand from creeping up into the belay device. If the climber descends too fast, let go of the lever to immediately stop the climber, but keep the brake hand secure.

Although the assisted-braking device can improve the safety of a climbing team, it is not a substitute for attentive and vigilant belaying. Because the hand motions of feeding rope are different from using a tubular device, and because lowering involves more attention from the guide hand, practice and master belaying with an assisted-braking belay device before entrusting your partner's life to it.

Belaying with Other Devices

With any device, there is no substitute for vigilant belaying. All of the lead belay principles still apply, like always keeping the brake hand on the brake strand of the rope, proper body position, and diligent rope management. Pay special attention to any operator instructions provided by the belay device manufacturer.

KEEPING THE CLIMBER SAFE

The belayer's responsibilities extend beyond taking in slack, feeding out rope, and braking the climber in a fall. Positioned on the ground, the belayer has a different perspective on the safety of the climber.

Indoors, the belayer is often in a better position than the climber to assess the line a fall will take. Although the climber may control how she falls, the belayer's actions will dictate the length of the fall. One may think that the best fall is the shortest fall, but on overhangs and other protruding features, this is not always the case. For example, if a climber were to fall from ten feet above an overhang, with the last bolt five feet below her, a tight belay would send her slamming into the lip of the overhang. This scenario can be particularly dangerous if the climber's feet clear the overhang but her upper body does not. To prevent such a scenario, a belayer might give the climber a bit more slack to ensure that the climber clears the lip in the event of a fall. The objective of belaying is to catch the climber and prevent a ground fall, so be careful with excess slack, but sometimes a little more slack can help protect the climber.

Communication between the climber and the belayer is essential in keeping the team safe. In addition to the basic commands, it is the belayer's responsibility to let the climber know of potential dangers. Because of the climber's high level of stress and concentration as she moves up, potential hazards such as back-clipping, Z clipping, skipping draws, and back-stepping the rope can occur unnoticed by the climber. The belayer should communicate with the climber to let her know of these potential dangers in a calm, unpanicked manner.

PRECLIMB	
BELAYER	**CLIMBER**
Check belay device and rope attachment.	Check tie-in knot.
Confirm proper positioning.	Locate the first bolt.
Attach to anchor.	Identify potential clipping holds.
Flake the rope.	Assess the route.
Confirm open line of communication.	Confirm open line of communication.

DURING THE CLIMB	
BELAYER	**CLIMBER**
Manage the rope.	Manage the rope.
Respond before and w after clipping.	Choose secure clipping stances.
Monitor and adjust amount of slack.	Clip bolts or protection correctly.
Maintain a stable, responsive stance.	Properly clip final anchors.

PUTTING THE SYSTEM TOGETHER

Although lead belaying and climbing have been presented separately, the actions of one depend on the other. Working together is essential in safe climbing. Climbers have their own style, and partners may need to become accustomed to each other. Some climbers clip draws from low positions, requiring the belayer to feed a lot of

KEY EXERCISE: MOCK LEADING AND BELAYING

There is little room for mistakes when lead climbing or belaying, and learning how to do either in a situation with live consequences is not recommended. There are many factors involved in minimizing the climber's risk, so mock leading and belaying provide reasonable room for error while learning.

The Goal: Learn to simulate all the components of lead climbing and belaying in the most realistic situation possible. This is also the best scenario to practice lead falls in a controlled environment.

The Setup: With the lead belayer, set up to climb the lead route. In addition to tying in to the lead rope, also tie in to the top rope, managed by another belayer. When climbing the lead route, the top rope is available for added security, in case the lead climber or belayer has difficulty.

MOCK LEADING AND BELAYING EXERCISE

1. Go through the preclimb checklist in this section with the top-rope belayer.
2. Go through the preclimb checklist with the lead belayer.
3. Before climbing, decide which belayer will take and lower the climber.
4. The climber leads the route while on top-rope belay. This situation is "real" in every sense for the entire party.

CONSIDERATIONS

- If you are just beginning to lead climb and belay, the top rope should be the primary safety rope. Keep the top-rope belay snug, so if the climber falls or needs to rest, he does not take a lead fall.
- When both belayers and the climber are comfortable, reach a consensus within the group that the lead belay is the primary safety rope. In this case, the top-rope belay must be loose enough to not interfere with a lead fall.
- As a climber, take realistic falls between bolts. Start with letting go with the last bolt clipped near the waist. As you feel more comfortable, take slightly longer falls. Do not skip bolts or take excessive falls.
- Accidents still happen when taking lead falls while mock leading. Check with the staff at your gym to see if they have any special conditions for taking lead falls.

If a lead route is too difficult for you to climb or you want to practice the moves and clipping positions before leading it, you can always top-rope a lead route that has already been led and unclip the quickdraws as you climb.

rope. Others may feel more comfortable clipping at their waist, where the belayer need not feed any rope to clip. Since these differences vary among climbers, attentive climbing and belaying make for a safer environment. There is no substitute for vigilant and attentive belaying. Climbing gyms afford many social distractions, but the sole purpose of the belayer is to focus on the safety and well-being of the climber.

As with all technical skills, perfect practice is the only way to ensure safety while lead climbing and belaying. Practicing the key exercises will better prepare climbers for the decision-making and adversity of lead climbing. Not only should the climber and belayer achieve a comfort level in their roles, but they must also be able to assess their actions and subsequent results. It is not enough to simply "lead and belay" correctly. The ability to logically assess situations and make informed, smart decisions is just as important. The belayer and climber have both individual and shared responsibilities before and during a climb (see the sidebar, p. 160, for checklists for both parties).

FOLLOWING A LEAD ROUTE

After finishing a lead route and safely reaching the ground again, the lead rope travels from the ground, up the wall through the draws, through the anchors, and hangs back down to the ground. To retrieve the rope, either pull the rope down, or allow a climber to "clean" the route.

When pulling the rope down, start from the end of the rope directly underneath the first bolt. If you pull the rope through the other side, the end will free-fall from the anchors, potentially harming you or someone else as it falls to the ground. If using a figure-eight retrace, immediately untie the initial figure eight from the rope so it does not get caught in the anchors.

If you opt to have a second climber to clean the route, the hanging lead rope is essentially a top rope with the climber's side of the rope clipped to carabiners. However, the rope must be clipped in to the anchors, since these are the same anchors for the second climber to top-rope on. If the lead climber did not clip the anchors, then pull the rope down.

The second climber ties in to the end of rope traveling to the first bolt, and the belayer attaches himself to the free end touching the ground. In general, do not tie in to the free-hanging end of the rope, particularly on steep or wandering routes. Falls will pendulum the climber out of control, endangering him and anyone else nearby. Once you are set up, the safety checks and commands are the same as for any other top-rope climb. The only difference is that the climber must unclip the rope from each carabiner as he reaches them. Obviously, the anchors remain untouched, and the climber should not climb above them. Before pulling the rope through the anchors after the climber finishes and lowers from the route, announce "Rope" to any nearby climbers in anticipation of its free fall from the anchors.

THE SHARP END

The "sharp end" of the rope is the lead end. By being on the sharp end in the gym, you've opened up all the available wall space. This freedom allows you to push your limits, work on your weaknesses, and celebrate your strengths. As you become more proficient at and comfortable with lead climbing and belaying, do not let down your guard. A climber and belayer rarely antici-pate a foot slipping off the wall or a handhold spinning, but with vigilant and attentive belaying, surprises won't turn into accidents.

Opposite: *Peak performance is sought not just by professionals, but by anyone who wants to reach their full potential.*

Performance

The joy and excitement a new climber experiences after reaching the top of a beginner's wall can equal that experienced by an elite climber completing a 5.14. Both climbers are motivated by the personal challenges their route presents and the satisfaction of rising to meet those challenges. Sometimes, joy of movement is enough, but for a lot of climbers, seeking challenging routes is part of the appeal of climbing.

As a climber's ability improves, different challenges unfold. The quest to master an activity drives improvement, and that desire comes from dedication to and enjoyment of the activity. As with most things in life, the more time, energy, and effort put into the activity, the richer the results. Climbing performance, or the way we function while carrying out the act of climbing, is a product of our investment in time, energy, and effort.

There are many factors that contribute to overall climbing performance. A climber may have impeccable technique, but a lack of mental tactics might limit overall performance. Or a physically strong climber's sloppy technique may be a barrier to improvement. To reach your full potential, physical conditioning, mental approach, and technique must all blend together for optimal climbing performance.

Although every climber experiences a different learning curve, or rate of improvement, reaching a performance plateau is inevitable. Even the most elite climbers have reached plateaus getting to the 5.15 grade. Some climbers accept their lack of improvement and continue climbing with the same level of enthusiasm. For these climbers, it is impossible to admit that they will not improve, because at any level, steps toward improvement are always available. Even the most elite climbers have room for improvement, though they must exert proportionally more effort than novice or intermediate climbers for even small gains in improvement. The challenge is in deciding whether an attempt at improvement is worth the time and effort.

This chapter addresses the four factors of performance: technical skill, mental approach, physical conditioning, and scheduling and periodization. Extensive time, energy, and research have been put into each of these pillars of climbing performance. There are specialists and institutions focused entirely on each of these topics and conduct countless physiological, biomechanical, and psychological studies. This chapter is designed to give you an introduction to these topics and set a solid foundation of how these all contribute to your overall climbing performance. Evaluating these factors can help you identify the areas that need the most attention.

TECHNICAL SKILL

Climbing movement is covered in-depth in Chapter 3, Movement Technique. This factor of performance should be mastered before focusing too much time and effort on the other aspects of performance. Climbing is such a movement-specific activity that learning how to travel properly is the foundation of any climber's success. In addition to performing the movement technique key exercises in this book and mastering those skills, doing so with the guidance of an instructor is invaluable. An experienced technique instructor has the ability to analyze your movement and point out the weak links in your armor. While your belayer or climbing partner can give you objective feedback, subjective pointers may be overlooked. Bad habits are hard to break, so it is important to have your climbing evaluated at the beginning of your climbing career and periodically

thereafter to ensure that your technique is sound.

FEEDBACK AND COACHING

Video analysis can be a valuable tool. You probably know more about your partner's climbing technique than your own, since the only analysis of your own climbing movement is subjective, based on how you feel. You may not realize that you chalk up excessively before every crux, drag your right foot against the wall when your left foot is high-stepping, or pump your feet a few times before committing to small footholds. Watching a recording of yourself along with an evaluation by an experienced instructor gives you an essential perspective on your climbing. If your gym's services do not include video analysis, have someone (not your belayer) grab a recording on a cell phone.

DELIBERATE PRACTICE

According to Anders Ericsson, a leading psychologist in expert performance, deliberate practice, up to ten thousand hours specifically, makes a performer an expert. This is not to say that ten thousand hours of climbing will make you an expert. As mentioned in Chapter 3, "perfect practice makes perfect." Deliberate practice is engaging in a mental or physical activity with a goal of improving performance. The practice could be working through the key exercises in this book, reflecting on feedback from a coach, or working on your weaknesses. These actions must be intentional and slightly stretch the bounds of your skill level. The

Having a coach, or personalized instruction, will help you identify weaknesses in your technique and turn them into strengths.

only real constraint on improvement and mastery is motivation.

We have a tendency to climb terrain that suits our strengths. For instance, if your forte is steep routes, your route selection will gravitate toward routes of that nature. If your movement skills on less-than-vertical climbs are not regularly used, your proficiency on that terrain will decline. Simply put, use it or lose it. Even if being a well-rounded climber is not important to you, to climb well at any grade requires a diverse bag of tricks.

MENTAL APPROACH

Your mental state is a powerful tool that is as trainable as the rest of your body. Goal setting, visualization, and maintaining self-confidence are all mental tasks or issues that affect how the body performs during a climb. Even the way in which you approach climbing and how you schedule your climbing sessions significantly affect performance.

At an elite level of performance, mental strength separates athletes from one another. Physically, they can be quite similar, but differences in performance are attributable to their mental approaches. Elite athletes are not the only ones to use mental training tactics to improve performance. Every climber should pay attention to how the mind affects the body. The central nervous system is a direct physical link between the mind and the body. What you think affects how your body reacts.

Altering your mental approach does not automatically improve climbing performance. The goal of mental training is to create a psychological state that sets the stage for optimal performance. The most advantageous mental state and the steps to achieve that state vary by the individual. Consider the following aspects that can help create a mental state conducive for climbing performance.

PRECLIMB ROUTINES

Preclimb routines can improve your mental state by telling your mind and body that climbing is about to commence. Something as simple as a couple of specific stretches or retying your climbing-shoe laces can prepare you for the challenge at hand. You may notice that you have already integrated some preclimb safety routines, such as commands with your belayer or spotter. Use these as mental cues to clear your mind and focus on your route or boulder problem.

CONTROLLABLE FACTORS

It is hard to push your limits while worrying about the competency of your belayer, whether or not anyone is spotting you, or how well your climbing shoes were resoled. Before actually climbing, deal with any issues that may distract you. You can only concentrate on so many things at one time, and you will generally climb at your best if all you are focused on the movement itself.

BREATHING

High-intensity climbing often leaves climbers breathless once back on the ground. The breathlessness is not because the climbing was aerobically taxing, like running or swimming. In actuality, climbers tend to hold their breath or take shallow breaths during heightened states of arousal or physical exertion. The breathlessness climbers experience hinders performance by limiting oxygen flow and increasing muscular tension throughout the body.

Rather than simply trying to remember to breathe, make a concerted effort to take a few deep abdominal breaths when resting or chalking up on a climb. Start with a complete exhalation, contracting the stomach to squeeze all the air out. The next breath should start by filling the lower abdomen with air and continue the breath into the chest. After a few breaths, the body will be more relaxed, oxygenated, and ready to climb.

MUSIC

You can guide your psychological state by listening to music. Just like upbeat, rhythmic tunes make you want to dance and lullabies put a baby to sleep, music can affect your climbing. If you find yourself bringing the stresses of work with you to the gym, consider reducing your tension by listening to something that soothes you and alters your mood. It is no coincidence that climbing gyms pump out upbeat tunes from their stereos.

You may choose to boulder with headphones and listen to your own music. This can help you stay motivated, but keep the volume low enough that you can hear other climbers and boulderers around you. Because it impedes communication with your belayer, never use headphones while route climbing.

MAINTAINING A POSITIVE APPROACH

An old saying says, essentially, "Whether you think you can or can't, you're probably right." It demonstrates the power of positive thinking and permeates all aspects of life, not just climbing. Maintain a positive approach to climbing at all levels. From having the confidence to set lofty goals to believing that you can reach the next handhold, a positive look at the end result will affect the outcome. A pessimistic view of climbing and your abilities will hurt your performance and, ultimately, your enjoyment of the activity.

VISUALIZATION

Visualization is a powerful practice that can significantly affect climbing performance. Seeing yourself perform at a desired level or executing moves in your mind convinces the body that your desired level of performance or those movements are possible, even if they are unlikely.

When you are attempting a new route, effective visualization depends on the your ability to sequence the moves of a climb. If you sequence the route incorrectly and then visualize it incorrectly, you may be setting yourself up for failure. For sections that appear tricky, visualize alternative moves in case the primary sequence proves impractical. Identifying difficult or tricky moves and then mentally rehearsing them

with perfect climbing technique can be done from either an external or internal perspective.

External Imagery

For an external approach to visualization, picture yourself being filmed by a camera facing the wall while you are on a route. As you look at the route in your mind, step back so that you can see as much as possible. Visualize yourself standing on the ground, starting with your preclimb routine. See yourself starting to climb in real time, and try to go through the entire route in a continuous manner from top to bottom. Picture everything that may happen: clipping carabiners on a lead climb, finding places to rest, down-climbing and trying different options at the crux, and clipping the anchors. Pay attention to parts of the visualization that become fuzzy or broken. This often indicates an unclear section of the route.

The benefit of external visualization is seeing yourself in relation to the entire route and envisioning success prior to your first attempt. With enough external imagery practice, you will develop a clear understanding of your spatial awareness relative to the route, which is helpful in gauging the distance between holds and whether you will be able to reach them.

Internal Imagery

Visualizing the climb from an internal approach allows your body and mind to prepare for the climb. Imagine the climb through your own eyes, as if you were on

Seeing the movement first in your mind is a good start to visualizing a climb before doing it.

the route. Be aware of how close the wall will feel to you on different moves, what that next foothold might look like when you are looking down and trying to step onto it, or how far the quickdraw is from your head when you are scrunched up in the roof and trying to clip it. If done right and backed up with external body awareness, you should be able to "feel" the moves before you actually get on the route.

Internal imagery is a key to success after your first attempt on a route. Because you have already attempted the route, the difficult moves have been identified. For example, perhaps you have been falling on a move that requires a strenuous twistlock and a long reach with your left hand. You have done the move a few times by itself but fall every time you attempt the entire route.

Mentally rehearse these moves sitting or reclined in a comfortable, quiet place with no distractions. Physically disassociate yourself from the high-energy climbing gym or bouldering cave. Close your eyes and focus on relaxing all the muscles in your body. Start with your head and work all the way down to your feet. Once relaxed, visualize yourself in a comfortable position just before the strenuous twistlock on your route. See yourself climbing up to the crux, and pay attention to your body relative to the route, like how close your hips should be from the wall, where the footholds are, or how much weight is on your right hand. Make sure your breathing is smooth and controlled. Now, start to move through the crux,

focusing on not only how the moves look from your perspective on the route but also how your body feels. Feel the twist as your left hip rotates toward the wall, the pressure on your toes as they push in opposition through the roof, and the way you reach for the hold with your left shoulder.

One of the significant factors of mental rehearsal is the ability to focus on the task at hand. You may visualize the crux moves and then realize that the grocery list or taking the cat to the vet has crept into your thoughts. Start small, as with focusing on the crux moves of the route. As your ability to focus improves, mentally rehearse longer sections of the route.

GOAL SETTING

Goal setting is a valuable step toward improvement. If you do not know your destination, it is difficult to plan for the journey. Due in part to the grading scale in climbing, most climbers define improvement as tackling routes or boulder problems at progressively harder grades. However, improvement can also include aspects of climbing, such as feeling more comfortable lead climbing, getting into the gym more often, or participating in a climbing competition. Whatever your form of improvement is, attaching a measurable outcome to it will help you more easily see the steps toward success. When planning these types of big-picture, long-term goals, think of what you would like to achieve. Setting long-term goals can help keep you focused on the ultimate task.

Short-term goals are the building blocks in achieving long-term success. By providing achievement steps that are appropriate to your skill level, short-term-goal success provides (relatively) instant gratification that promotes seeking your long-term goal. For example, if one of your big-picture goals is to lead 5.10 in the gym, and you are currently a 5.10 climber on top rope with new lead skills, start by building solid lead climbing skills, working your way through the easy and moderate grades as a leader, and then tackle 5.10 on lead. The sequence of goal setting is to continually break down the goals into the smallest pieces that can be easily managed and achieved. That way, you line your path to success with bite-sized tasks.

GRADES

To improve, a climber's skill level must be matched with a route to create an appropriate amount of challenge. Continually climbing on routes that are beyond your current skill level can keep you from learning the proper techniques for the moves at hand. In addition, constant failure on routes that are beyond your limit can create too much frustration, making you question your progress. At the same time, climbing too many easy routes can leave you mentally disengaged, eliminating the self-challenge of the activity.

Some climbers really enjoy attempting routes that they've never been on before and don't know anything about. This type of climbing is "on-sighting." You attempt the climb on-sight without any prior knowledge

of watching another climber or learning the "beta" (information). The first time on a route is your on-sight attempt. To climb a route on-sight is a true test of a climber's ability to sequence and read a route. Any attempt after the first try is a "redpoint" attempt. So there is a distinction between successfully climbing a route on your first attempt (on-sight) or having to "work" the route (redpoint).

Typically, a climber's hardest redpoint should be a full grade harder than what she can on-sight. For example, if the hardest grade you can on-sight is 11b, with enough time and effort, you probably have the skill set for 12b. That may require a few attempts or several, but as you remember the sequences and your body remembers the moves, the climbing will become easier. If the difference between your on-sight and redpoint abilities is less than a grade, let's say 11b on-sight and 11d redpoint, you may want to push yourself and get on harder routes to redpoint. If there's a wide discrepancy, like 11b on-sight and 12c redpoint, you may want to focus more on on-sighting skills.

The grades and number of routes between your on-sight and redpoint levels are also important. You want to build a solid foundation of on-sight skills and routes as you layer on harder routes. This wide foundation that tapers as the routes get harder is your climbing route "pyramid." This pyramid is directional and need not be taken literally, but the wider you build your pyramid, the easier it is to progress. In looking at the example pyramid shown,

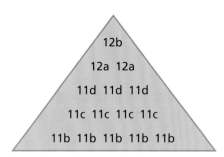

A solid progression pyramid for a climber who has redpointed 5.12b

if the climber wants to move on from 12b to climb 12c, he may want to climb another 11c, 11d, 12a, and 12b to add a foundation to the 12c.

CLIMBING PARTNERS

We all learn movement skills in different ways. Sight is most often used to gather information about and to learn movement skills. With this in mind, consider that who you climb with can affect personal improvement. If you are the most accomplished climber in your regular climbing group, your friends have the advantage of seeing how you perform moves and can take advice from you on their projects. It may be flattering to have your friends hold your climbing in high regard and always come to you for help, but your own improvement may suffer. Take time to climb with people whom you can learn from. Of course, this does not mean you should abandon your friends because they do not climb the grades you do. After all, who you climb with is an integral part of the experience. Nor should you climb with

people simply because they climb harder routes than you. Instead, seek climbers who have performance traits such as excellent technique on technical terrain or a strong mental game. Perhaps you and your climbing posse always choose overhanging terrain. A different climbing partner may have other preferences than what you are used to.

Take time to learn about your (potential) climbing partner's goals to see if the two of you are compatible. If she is an antisocial climbing machine who will not settle for fewer than twenty hard routes in a climbing session, and you just want to climb a few easy routes, keep looking. Even if the partner in question has passed his belay test, make sure that you feel comfortable having that person as a climbing partner.

PHYSICAL CONDITIONING

While movement technique is the foundation of climbing performance, the body must be able to perform the task at hand. Climbing-specific fitness, such as hand strength, can limit climbing improvement, but general fitness, such as core strength or weight management, also indirectly affects performance. Even if you know the correct body positioning, physical limitations can limit progress and even lead to injury. The main components of physical fitness for gym climbing are flexibility, muscular strength and endurance, and body composition. Lacking sufficient development in any of these areas can be a barrier to improvement.

FLEXIBILITY AND STRETCHING

A full range of joint, tendon, and muscular motion affects climbing performance and prevents injury. Tight tendons and ligaments limit the body's range of motion, can hinder proper body positioning while climbing, and may increase the risk of injury. Lower-body flexibility (or lack of it) is often noticed during high-steps, stemming, drop-knee moves, and climbing in the frontal position using the inside edge of the foot. Most climbers do not have problems with climbing-specific upper-body flexibility, although inflexible shoulders can hinder gaston moves and potentially lead to injury. Limitations in flexibility are most apparent where overdeveloped climbing-specific muscles impede nonclimbing range of motion.

Stretching, or deliberately moving your muscles or tendons in flexion or stretch, improves flexibility. Furthermore, stretching before climbing can improve performance and decrease the chance of injury. It is also possible to be too flexible. Excessively flexible climbers are susceptible to joint dislocations, primarily in the hip and shoulder sockets.

Flexibility can improve in as little as a month if stretches are performed at least twice a week. Hold all stretches for thirty seconds in a static position (no bouncing) that creates muscular tension without causing pain. Be sure to breathe while holding the stretch. To increase the depth of the stretch, gently intensify the force while exhaling. All the pictured stretches cover the muscle groups that are most relevant to climbing flexibility and can be done without a partner.

Upper Back and Shoulders

Bring your left arm across your chest, bending your arm slightly. Grab your left arm with your right hand just above the elbow, and gently pull to the right, stretching your left arm and shoulder. Repeat on the other side of your body.

Upper back and shoulder stretch

Stretching the arms, biceps, and chest

A great stretch to open up the chest

Arms, Biceps, and Chest

Stand with a wall to your right and extend your right arm to reach the wall. You can grab a large handhold if available. If using a blank wall, place the palm of your right hand firmly against it. To initiate the stretch, keep your arm straight, and slowly rotate your chest away from the wall. Keep your right shoulder low while stretching. This also can stretch the biceps and chest. Repeat on the other side of your body.

To stretch the chest further, stand next to a wall or column so that you can place your left elbow against the wall with your hand pointing up and palm against the wall. Your left elbow and chest should be in line with each other. Gently rotate your upper body to the right, so you feel the stretch on the left side the chest. Repeat on the other side of your body.

Fingers and Forearms

This first stretch is an excellent preclimb warm-up to get blood flowing through your forearms and to prepare your fingers for squeezing. Hold your left hand in front of your body with your arm extended and palm facing out. Grasp a fingertip with your right hand and gently pull your finger toward your body. After releasing, move on to your other fingers. This can also be performed grabbing multiple fingers of the same hand. Repeat on the other side of your body.

To stretch both forearms at the same time, place your palms together in front of your body. The heels of your hands should be in line with your elbows. Gently push your hands together while slowly rotating

This forearm stretch is useful between climbs and during training sessions.

Overhead triceps stretch

your fingertips away from you and down to point toward the ground. This is extremely effective postclimb but is also helpful during warm-up. This stretch can help prevent and relieve blood-filled "pumped" forearms.

Triceps

Raise your left arm above your head and bend your elbow, reaching your left hand down your back. Grasp your left elbow with your right hand, and push your left elbow down and slightly away from your back. Repeat on the other side of your body.

Hips

To improve your turnout, or your ability to rotate your toes and knees away from each other, stand with your feet shoulder-width apart and toes pointed out at a 45-degree angle. Keeping your upper body upright, slowly bend your knees and squat. To intensify the stretch, place your elbows on your knees and gently push out. You can also point your feet out farther to increase the intensity.

To loosen up your lower back, sit with your legs stretched in front of you. Cross one leg, knee bent, over the other, and put

Having mobile hips helps you keep your center of gravity close to the wall on vertical and less-than-vertical terrain.

This seated twist opens and stretches the lower back before steep climbing and twistlocking.

that foot outside your other thigh. Twist your torso toward the hip of your bent leg.

Hamstrings

For the seated forward bend, sit on the ground with your legs extended in front. Maintain a slight arch in your lower back with your torso in an upright position. Lean forward from your hips, reach forward with your hands and bring your chest toward your knees. To keep a slight arch in your lower back, bend your knees enough for your hands to touch your toes.

Neck

"Belayer's neck" is the term used for neck soreness from looking up too much at a climber while belaying. To help prevent

soreness, drop your head forward, and relax all the muscles in your neck. Then, gently and slowly rotate your head to the side. Stop the rotation when your head is tilted to the side, and then rotate your head to the other side and then back to the middle. The stretch can be intensified by placing a hand on top of your head to gently guide the range of motion.

MUSCULAR STRENGTH AND CONDITIONING

Climbers often state after failing on a route that they were "too weak" or "not strong enough." Most often, deficiencies in climbing technique sap their strength prematurely. However, there are instances in which climbing-specific strength can benefit your climbing. Keep in mind that strength training will make you a better climber only if you have a solid foundation in climbing technique. More strength is the worst substitute for movement skills. Powering through moves will not always work, especially on delicate terrain.

It is also important to understand the difference between strength and endurance. If when attempting a route you lack the ability to perform a single move, strength is the limiting factor. If you fall because your forearms are pumped with so much blood and lactic acid buildup that hand control is lost, then insufficient forearm muscular endurance is to blame. Understanding this difference is essential in identifying your weaknesses and in training to improve performance.

GENERAL MUSCULAR BALANCE
Training for muscular strength comprises muscular balance and climbing-specific strength. Developing climbing-specific strength focuses on the muscles of the upper body that pull, but every dedicated climber should consider training for overall muscular balance. Climbing, particularly bouldering and steep routes, requires a significant amount of pulling motion with the upper body. This action promotes strengthening of the biceps and shoulders. However, their counterparts, the triceps and chest, remain underdeveloped. This discrepancy in strength between weak triceps and strong biceps makes the elbows susceptible to pain while climbing. An underdeveloped

chest and strong shoulders can sway posture and lead to injury.

To promote muscular balance, non-climbing-specific exercises should be performed to strengthen these seldom-used muscles. Most strength-training exercises for climbers are performed under body weight, without traditional weights. The idea is to develop the strength needed to push and pull your own body weight against gravity, which is essentially climbing. "Pumping iron" can lead to excess bulk that might not translate very well to improving your strength-to-weight ratio. Common training tools for climbers are rings, pull-up bars, or hanging straps with adjustable handles.

There are a multitude of possibilities for exercises when training a specific muscle or group of muscles. The exercises shown here are those performed by our pros and have been successful for them. Proper form is particularly important with all of these exercises. Improper form renders the exercise ineffective and possibly dangerous. Have a personal trainer critique your exercises, or perform them in front of a mirror to ensure correct form.

As a starting point, perform two sets of repetitions to muscular failure. In other words, perform as many repetitions as you can at a steady pace while maintaining good form. Stop the exercises when your form deteriorates. Wait a few minutes, and then repeat the exercise until failure again. Perform these exercises two or three times a week after climbing.

Chest

Push-ups can be performed anywhere and do not require any special equipment. The resistance from this exercise comes from body weight. To work torso stability, the chest, shoulders, and triceps, lie on the floor with the toes firmly planted on the ground and palms placed just outside the shoulders. While pushing up, the back of the head, back, and legs should be in line with each other. Keep the head facing down to keep the neck from hyperextending. While keeping a straight line between the shoulders and heels through body tension, slowly lower the chest all the way to the floor, touching it if possible.

Placing the knees on the ground is a less stressful modification of the push-up. A narrower hand position, while keeping the elbows close to the body throughout the exercise, places more stress on the triceps.

Push-ups with ring stabilization

Push-ups can be made more difficult using a suspended ring system. This approach requires full-body stabilization and results in a greater overall workout.

Triceps

Effectively isolate the triceps with dip exercises. Using a stable chair or bench, sit on the very edge of it with the hands placed at the edge next to the hips. The heels of the feet should be on the ground with the legs straight. Push the hips from the bench and straighten the arms. Move the heels a few small steps away from the bench, moving the hips away, too. Keep the shoulders high to prevent them from sagging, and maintain a slight bend at the elbows. Although this exercise depends on your flexibility, lower your body until your upper arms are parallel to the floor. Keep the elbows pointed directly back to isolate the triceps. Then push back up to the starting position.

The exercise can be made easier by placing the hands and feet on the floor, although the range of motion will be limited. Intensify the exercise by placing the heels on a higher platform, such as another chair. Using rings to perform triceps dips (as shown) requires more stabilization. An ultimate range-of-motion excercise is the ring muscle-up. This advanced move engages the chest and core, requiring technique and strength.

Core

There simply cannot be enough emphasis on maintaining a strong core. All movement,

These ring dips target the triceps, but are a great upper-body stabilizer, too.

even subtleties, stems from the lower back, obliques, and abdomen. A tired lower back may result in sagging hips when they should be over your feet, or your feet may continually slip off of holds on steep terrain when your core isn't engaged. Countless crunches and sit-ups are limiting, so try exercises and movements that cover a broader range of motion.

A good place to start is with the basic plank. Assume a push-up position, with a straight line drawn through your head, shoulders, and hips. Dropping to your elbows will lower the intensity of the exercise. When holding the plank, breath smoothly, and focus on maintaining your posture until your form breaks. Intensify the plank by adding rings to give you an increased range of motion. While getting into the plank position, put both feet into rings positioned a foot off the ground. While holding the plank, bring your knees up your chest. Hold, and then return to the start position.

Another strong core-stabilization exercise is the kettlebell Russian twist, or half

These ringed plank crunches require a lot of core stabilization throughout the range of motion.

Choose heavier or lighter kettlebells to make these Russian twists harder or easier. The twisting motion builds core strength for steep climbing.

V twist. Sit on the ground with your legs out in front of you, knees raised enough to lift your feet off the ground. You can cross your feet if that's more comfortable. Grasp a kettlebell or other type of weight with both hands, and hold it above the ground on one side of your body. In a controlled manner, move the weight across your body to the other side, hovering above the ground, and repeat.

CLIMBING-SPECIFIC CONDITIONING

Inefficient technique can make a climber feel like lack of strength is the limiting factor in climbing performance. However, even with perfect climbing technique, there comes a time when strength *is* a limiting factor. That strength limitation is often felt in the hands, arms, shoulders, back, and core. While general conditioning, as addressed in the previous section, provides overall fitness, climbing-specific conditioning targets muscles and develops strength that directly translates to climbing movement.

A common misconception is that climbing, alone, will strengthen climbing-specific muscles. This is true to a limited extent. To develop strength, the muscle must be stressed and then allowed to rest. As the muscles adapt to the stress, they becomes stronger, and more stress can be applied for additional strength gains. By simply climbing, strength will develop and then eventually plateau since the amount of weight on the hands (body weight) is constant. To continue to develop strength, you need to train your climbing-specific muscles harder than you can actually climb. There are a few commonly used training methods that have proven very successful for developing climbing-specific strength, and most are integrated into climbing gym design.

Hangboards

A hangboard is an essential training tool for upper-body conditioning and developing hand strength and endurance. Given the choice between training with a hangboard or any other type of hand-strengthening tools or exercises, choose hangboards. Hangboards are superior because of their specificity to climbing movement and the strength needed to perform that movement.

Manufactured hangboards are made out of either the same material as artificial handholds or wood. Wooden boards are friendlier on the skin for extended sessions and training. These training tools are about as wide as your shoulders and are sculpted with multiple grips, from handlebar jugs to "barely there" slopers. The most basic hangboard has various-sized edges and slopers, while more intricate hangboards have multiple pockets and pinches. Just about every climbing gym in the nation has mounted a hangboard, but their compact size, reasonable price, and mounting ease make them attractive to have at home. It is possible to make your own hangboard by mounting pairs of identical holds about shoulder-width apart. The best place to mount a hangboard is above a doorjamb so that there is room for your body to comfortably hang freely.

Training Walls

Stemming from the concept of deliberate practice, training walls are designed to focus on specific moves. They tend to not be very tall and are densely packed with climbing holds to allow for maximum hold choices in a limited amount of space. The angle of these walls is often adjustable to allow for variable difficulty. Holds can be the same as you would find on the climbing walls or a wooden variety. Different types of walls with different training focuses are discussed later in this chapter.

HANGBOARD UPPER-BODY CONDITIONING

There is a distinction between training for upper-body strength and grip strength using a hangboard. Hand-strength training focuses on the force and size of the holds being gripped, with the upper body in a "dead hang," whereas upper-body strength engages the upper arms, shoulders, and back, often through a range of motion. The primary upper-body-conditioning exercise on a hangboard is a pull-up, which engages the biceps, shoulders, and back. Because the focus is working upper-body muscles specifically, use the biggest holds. The goal is to work the biceps, shoulders, and upper back to muscular failure, not the hands and forearms.

The more repetitions performed, the more muscular endurance is trained. Modify the exercises for a more strength-oriented workout by adding a weight belt, and limit the number of repetitions to less than five. Your current fitness level dictates whether or not an exercise promotes muscular strength or endurance. For example, if you can perform eight pull-ups, then those pull-ups are developing muscular endurance. If your partner can do only three, his exercises are helping him develop strength.

The following upper-body exercises are listed from least to most demanding. For the best results, meet the first exercise's recommended set before moving on to the next exercise.

Lock-Offs

Start with your hands on the largest holds and either jump up or use a spotter or chair to position your chest as high as possible on the board. After shifting all your weight to your hands, maintain the position for as long as possible. Make sure to keep your chest high on the hangboard. Rest for about a minute and repeat again. Work up to three sets of twenty to thirty seconds each.

Lock-Off Lowers

Start in the same position as the basic lock-off. As soon as your hands are fully weighted, slowly lower yourself in a controlled manner to full arm extension. If using a chair, make sure it is out of the way during the lowering stage. Step down, rest for about a minute, and repeat again. Work up to three sets of lock-off lowers, taking ten to twenty seconds to lower.

Pull-Ups

Start with your hands on the most comfortable holds, arms fully extended and feet lifted off the ground. Raise your chest as

Adding weight to pull-ups develops maximum strength rather than endurance.

high as possible (hand height), and then lower back to the starting position. Focus on stabilizing your body to keep from swinging. For maximum control, pull up on a two-second count and lower on a four-second count. Work up to three sets of six to fifteen pull-ups. Add weight to limit the number of pull-ups to failure, as shown.

Typewriter Lock-Off

Start in the lock-off position, with your chin pulled up above the hangboard. From here, move your chest laterally, touching it (or your chin, which is a bit easier) to your hand. Alternate touching hands as many times as possible.

Typewriter Pull-Ups

Typewriter pull-ups are a more difficult variation. From a hanging position, move your chest to the right, pull up, typewriter over to the left, and then lower on the left side. Then repeat by moving up the left side, over to the right, and then down.

HANGBOARD HAND STRENGTH AND CONDITIONING

Climbing would be a different experience if every hold felt like a jug and your hands never fatigued. Hangboard exercises for hand strength and endurance might not make those dreams come true, but they will help you hold on to bad holds for longer amounts of time. A majority of the muscles responsible for moving the hand and creating grip strength are located in the forearms, which connect to the fingers via tendons and ligaments. Therefore, forearm and hand strength are closely related. This is why forearm size and definition can help you pick out the climbers at a party.

The Dead Hang for Endurance

Dead hangs are used for the bulk of hand conditioning. While the name makes it sound like you hang like a sack of bricks, it's very important to keep your upper body engaged, with a slight raise in the chest and external rotation in the shoulders. Stand on a chair if you cannot reach the hangboard, then grab a pair of holds. An open-hand grip promotes forearm strength more than crimping and is easier on the joints and tendons. Once you are settled, pick your feet up and hang from the holds for as long as possible. Engage your shoulders, keeping your chest slightly elevated and preventing your upper body from slumping between your arms. Perform three sets of dead hangs, resting for about a minute between each hang.

Once you can hold on for at least thirty seconds, consider using more difficult holds. For each hang, grab a different pair of holds. If you always use the same holds, your hands will develop endurance for that exact position, so vary the grip. Do three to five repetitions of up to thirty-second-long hangs with grip A, rest a few minutes, and then do three to five repetitions of up to thirty-second-long hangs with grip B.

GUIDELINES FOR HAND-STRENGTH CONDITIONING

- Long hangs (greater than ten seconds) to muscular failure develop muscular endurance.
- Short hangs (five to ten seconds) to muscular failure develop muscular strength.
- Alter the hang time by changing the weight or the holds.
- Vary the holds to increase your hands' ranges of motion.
- Use an open-hand grip to develop forearm strength and decrease the risk of injury.

Proper hangboard technique keeps the shoulders engaged and chest and upper body slightly raised—not sagging.

The Dead Hang for Strength

Training for hand strength with dead hangs is similar to training for endurance, but the intensity changes. While endurance hangs are held for up to thirty seconds, hangs promoting strength should reach failure in only five to ten seconds. Adding weight increases the intensity of the exercise by overstressing the muscles.

Finding the right combination of hold type and added weight takes some experimentation. A sign of increased hand strength is the ability to hang on for relatively longer amounts of time on the same holds. When you can hang on for longer than ten seconds, add weight. Remember to vary your grip.

Do three to five repetitions of up to five to ten seconds with grip A, rest a few minutes, and then do three to five repetitions of up to five to ten seconds with grip B.

TRAINING WALLS FOR CLIMBING POWER AND ENDURANCE

Movement is initiated by muscular strength. This strength is defined as the maximum amount of force generated by a muscle or group of muscles. However, there are different aspects of strength as it relates to climbing. A climber has a given amount of strength, but the number of times or the speed with which that strength can be applied greatly affects climbing performance. To improve strength, it is important to recognize the distinctions between power, endurance, and anaerobic endurance and to train accordingly.

Power

A powerful climber possesses the ability to perform explosive moves. By definition, power is the amount of work performed divided by the time it takes to perform the work. Using two identical climbers doing the same move as an example, the one who performs the move faster generates more power. Power is often the precursor to dynamic movement, since the initial speed generated carries the climber to the desired holds.

Consider a climber on a route that has a tough move on it, perhaps at a roof. The route, say a 5.12, may contain mostly 5.11 climbing but have a single 5.12 crux move at this roof. If the climber is not able to perform the move, even after ample rest on the rope and using good movement technique, he lacks the necessary power to climb the route.

Bouldering

High-intensity climbing through bouldering improves muscular power. The training method for developing power is to engage in short bursts of high-intensity work followed by ample rest. Through bouldering, you can climb a few moves at your limit, then immediately rest.

Although many climbers who enjoy roped climbing stay away from bouldering areas since they do not see themselves as boulderers, it is impossible to develop muscular power without performing moves at your limit, and bouldering provides this opportunity. Climbing for power should come at the beginning of a workout, while

High-intensity bouldering is a powerful way to generate strength and explosive movement.

the muscles are still fresh and capable of producing 100 percent effort. Take extreme care to properly warm up before a high-intensity bouldering session.

Boulderers training for power should attempt problems four to eight moves long. The rest interval between attempts should be long enough that a forearm pump is not noticeable at the start of the next attempt. An excellent bouldering workout is choosing a problem on which you can do a few of the moves. Attempt the problem, and note where you fall (if you do not fall, the problem is obviously too easy). After some rest, get back on the problem at the same spot where you fell to work out the moves. Continue the process until you complete the problem. You can then continue to a new problem, or, better yet, repeat the same problem.

While bouldering alone can help you develop power, it's difficult to accurately measure and identify specific weaknesses and improvements. Even within the same bouldering grade, each problem requires a different set of skills, techniques, and strengths. It's difficult to systematically and measurably increase intensity and make improvements, as well as develop bilateral strength. This is where training walls come into play. With training walls, you're no longer climbing what a route setter has created for you but training specific climbing movements to uncover, and strengthen, your weaknesses.

System Wall

A system wall is purpose-built to promote incremental and measurable gain in climbing movement and strength. The wall is only high enough for two or three moves up on each side of the body. The basic idea is that the climbing holds are mirrored (to the left and right from the middle), and the angle of the wall can be changed. The two features serve two distinct functions.

The mirrored setting of holds means that you can perform the exact same movements on both sides of your body. For instance, if you grab a right-hand sloper and move the left hand to a high pocket, then there will also be a left-hand sloper for you to grasp as you move your right hand to a high pocket. The ability to perform moves on both sides of your body will point out any functional weaknesses you might have on one side. Identifying these weak points is the first step toward improvement.

The steeper the angle, the more body tension (fingertips to toes) is required to stay on the wall. Systematically increasing the wall angle makes the movement incrementally harder. This makes monitoring improvement more accurate. Because the movements are measurable (specific holds and angle of the wall), the idea is to perform repeated moves, building a progression of difficulty over time. Once you

Tapping into the science of training, system walls allow you to train deliberately and focus on your weaknesses and areas that need improvement.

develop the strength and movement to do move A, B, C at 25 degrees, you progress to doing A, B, C at 30 degrees, and so on. Other than angle, other factors that affect intensity are the size of the holds, the resting intervals, the length of moves (distance between holds), and the length of time to do a move (climbing more statically and slowly). To see real gains, you need to perform the exercise over multiple weeks and on a regular basis. It's important to add variety to the movement. Changing the

movement every four weeks is enough time to make improvement but also keep the kinesthetic learning fresh.

There are several variations of the system wall, but they're all rooted in the idea of executing a few explosive moves on an overhanging wall. Some have fixed angles that do not adjust, while other training walls lack mirrored holds. Moon Boards, developed by training and climbing legend Ben Moon, have exact specifications in terms of size, angle, hold type, and

Matt generates maximum upper-body muscle fiber recruitment through a footless campus workout.

configuration. Using a Moon Board, climbers can train systematically with global standards through an online community.

Campus Board

While Wolfgang Gullich trained for the first ascent of *Action Directe* (5.14d) in the early 1990s, he devised a training wall with wooden rungs and no footholds on his college campus. Campus board training is an advanced technique and should be performed by climbers who have reached a performance plateau and have been climbing for at least two years. Because of the extreme dynamic forces put on the fingers and upper body, the climber's tendons and ligaments need to be strong enough to endure the exercises without injury.

The training principle behind campus board training, or "campusing," is shock-loading the fingers by moving up and down on wooden rungs without using your feet. Your body weight is supported entirely by your fingertips while you bound up and down the campus board. This training improves contact strength, or the ability for your fingers to generate strength quickly as the fingertips land on each hold.

Start off slow with the campus board. First, treat the rungs like a hangboard, hanging from the rungs with proper posture. Next, practice moving one hand up one rung and then back down, using footholds if available. This exercise will require not only physical strength but hand-eye coordination as well. Only after feeling comfortable and working up to this stage should you start to use the campus board

moving hand over hand and skipping rungs. Campusing is extremely taxing on the body and requires up to two days of resting for full recovery.

There are also variations of the campus board that work the upper body (arms, shoulders, and back) more than the fingers. These systems use peg-boards, handlebar holds, or other easy-to-grab grips.

Endurance

The ability to generate strength multiple times is muscular endurance. A climber with exceptional endurance never tires. If a climber falls off a route near the top because she simply could not hold on anymore, endurance is the limitation. Most likely, her forearms are pumped, and after she rests and lets the pump subside, the moves suddenly feel much easier. A 5.10 endurance route could consist solely of 5.9 moves, but the route may be long enough that it feels like 5.10.

To improve endurance, climb at a low intensity but for much longer than power training. By performing at a lower intensity, the muscles never work to their fullest capacity, and lactic acid production is kept at bay. If the intensity of endurance training gets too high, then an overproduction of lactic acid compromises the duration of the workout.

Endurance improves with long bouts of continuous climbing at low to moderate intensity. For example, climbing up and down an easy to moderate route is an excellent way to improve climbing endurance. If possible, try to rest on the route, looking for stems, knee bars, or heel hooks. Choose terrain that allows fifteen to thirty minutes of uninterrupted climbing. This can be awfully boring for a belayer, so consider using auto-belay mechanisms (if provided in the gym) or traversing in the bouldering area. System walls can also be good for training endurance since you won't be interrupting other climbers trying to get on boulder problems or routes. If you have trouble staying on the wall without falling while working up to fifteen minutes or more, just get back on the wall after thirty seconds of rest so that your cumulative wall time is fifteen to thirty minutes. Staying on the wall for that much time can become tedious, so consider keeping your mind occupied with technique drills or by paying special attention to different aspects of your movement.

Anaerobic Endurance

Between the ends of the power and endurance spectrum lies anaerobic endurance, or power endurance. A route requiring both power and endurance has sections of difficult moves surrounded by moderate climbing or has sustained moves throughout the climb. A 5.11 anaerobic-endurance route comprises multiple 5.11 moves. Because of the dual strength demand, it brings out the best (or worst) of both power and endurance climbing.

Developing anaerobic endurance. Whereas power training involves high intensity and short duration, and endurance demands low intensity and long duration, anaerobic endurance is somewhere in between. Anaerobic endurance can be improved by using roped routes or bouldering. Assessing the true difficulty of each move of a boulder problem is easier than on a roped route, so bouldering is a more accurate means of training for anaerobic endurance. If you do train for anaerobic endurance on routes, look for those with a consistent difficulty of moves.

Consider the 4x4 bouldering workout: Choose four problems that you have done on-sight. Climb the first problem, wait a rest interval of two minutes, and then repeat this cycle three more times. Follow this with a five-minute rest, and then proceed to the second problem. Climb the second problem in the same fashion as the first. Continue with problems three and four. Minimizing the rest intervals between attempts puts more emphasis on endurance. Increasing the difficulty of the problems (and lengthening the rest interval) creates a more power-oriented workout. Performing the 4x4 workout on routes focuses more on the endurance side of the spectrum, so be prepared for a major pump!

BODY COMPOSITION

A common view of body composition compares the proportion of fat stores, muscle, and bone. Once you stop growing, bone mass is constant, but the amount of muscle and fat tissue can change. Gains in strength result from increases in muscle fiber recruitment and in the actual size of the muscle. However, bigger is not necessarily better, since too much muscle can limit range of motion and can be dead weight if in the wrong place.

Since fat stores are not a primary source of energy for most gym and rock climbers, excess fat also acts as dead weight, constantly pulling the climber down. Excess calories convert to fat stores when you take in more calories than you expend through exercise. While it is important that everyone maintain a healthy level of body fat (5–18 percent for active adult males, 16–33 percent for active adult females), excess stores not only limit climbing performance, but impose general health risks as well.

Climbing with a five-pound weight tied to your waist all the time impedes your strength-to-weight ratio, and excess fat stores are no different than that weight. Using pull-ups to explain strength-to-weight ratio, the heavier you are, the more strength is needed to perform the exercise. Excess weight alters your center of gravity and hinders body positioning and flexibility. A sensible diet and aerobic exercise are healthy ways to manage body composition.

AEROBIC EXERCISE

Aerobic exercise improves metabolism and burns excess food stores. Continuous exercise that uses large muscles in a rhythmic fashion—such as running, cycling, swimming, or cross-country skiing—burns more calories than stop-and-go activities such as climbing. You can burn excess fat stores and improve blood and oxygen flow with cardiovascular workouts. Even just a little bit of aerobic exercise a week goes a long way in terms of improvement.

Try working out two times a week for at least thirty minutes per session. The true path to aerobic fitness is training three to five days a week at twenty to sixty minutes per session. In terms of total energy expenditure, high-intensity workouts (fast running) for a short amount of time can equal a lower-intensity workout (slow jogging) for a long amount of time. With this in mind, the duration of your workout depends on its intensity.

SCHEDULING AND PERIODIZATION

If a climber came into the gym twice a week, every week, for a year, and climbed eight routes every time of about the same grade, he would improve some, but then his performance would plateau. Not only that, but climbing the same workouts in such a monotonous fashion is so boring that he may lose interest in climbing altogether. Periodization training, or variations in intensity, specificity, and volume of training, is a key element when training for climbing. Some climbers may periodize their training to coincide with an outdoor climbing road trip, the summer season, or a competition. Others may periodize their training around a specific goal. A periodized training cycle is recommended for climbers who have already developed sound climbing technique and whose performance gains have reached a plateau.

A periodization cycle is designed to allow the climber's performance to peak at certain times or events, often coinciding with set goals. Because the timeline of attaining that goal may be a week to several years, a periodization cycle could cover that same time range. A long periodization cycle consists of smaller cycles that are repeated and altered to meet the desired outcome. A common cycle is twelve weeks. This cycle is long enough to make a significant difference in climbing ability but not too long that the climber loses interest or becomes too fatigued. In addition, four of these cycles conveniently fit into a year, along with some rest time. Within a twelve-week cycle are several smaller cycles, designed to work on the components of endurance, power endurance, and power.

A DELIBERATE CLIMBING SESSION

The smallest component of a climbing periodization schedule is a single climbing session. Just like with an overall periodization cycle, the order and blend of intensity, volume, and specific exercises mold performance. Within a climbing session, warming up, working on technique and skill, performing a focus set, and cooling down all contribute to a meaningful workout designed to help achieve climbing goals.

Warming Up

The tone of a climbing session is set at the warm-up. An improper warm-up can leave you feeling stiff while climbing and can increase the risk of injury, whereas an adequate warm-up prepares your body for the rigors to follow. The primary functions of warming up are to elevate body temperature and to lengthen the muscles and ligaments, which decreases the risk of injury and can help improve performance. A warm-up comprises general and climbing-specific components.

An example of a general warm-up is stretching, calisthenics, or a cardiovascular activity such as running. While these activities are not performed while climbing, doing them prior to your workout improves general blood flow and muscle temperature. An aerobic preclimb workout not only is an adequate warm-up but also helps weight management. Perform the stretches described earlier in this chapter as well, paying special attention to any muscle groups that may be exceptionally tight or sore.

Easy climbing is the climbing-specific component of warming up. Climb a route below your current on-sight level. If you on-sight 5.11, consider warming up on a 5.9 or 5.10. During the climb, focus on moving slowly and in control. Gently overexaggerate moves like twistlocks or weight shifts for an extended range of motion that will further increase flexibility. Since the climb is easy, take plenty of time completing it while focusing on footwork and body positioning.

A climbing-specific warm-up avoids the dreaded forearm "flash pump." When a climber grips holds, the hands constantly squeeze and relax, an action initiated by the muscles in the forearms. As the hand squeezes or weights a hold, a by-product of the muscle contraction (lactic acid) develops in the forearms. Because the muscle fibers have contracted, cutting off the blood from leaving the arms, the lactic acid builds. Enough lactic acid buildup leaves the forearms pumped and unable to properly contract and relax the hands. Easy climbing warms up the forearms by allowing a gentle contraction-and-relaxation cycle, preparing the muscles for more intense gripping later. Once a climber gets a flash pump by climbing too intensely without warming up, the detrimental effects can stay with the climber for the rest of the day.

Skill and Technique Refinement

Deliberately working on climbing skills and techniques is the fastest way to improvement. Because your body is not yet tired and your mind is still fresh, learn and reinforce new skills at the beginning of workout sessions. If working on movement skills, now is the time to practice key exercises, have a trainer evaluate your movement, or experiment with new types of moves. This is also the time to practice technical skills, such as lead climbing or belaying or spotting. Working on skill and technique is not imperative to every climbing session, but if you do choose to work on them, do so right after the warm-up.

Focus Set

This is where the "just climb" part of the climbing session fits in; a focus set is the actual climbing you do during a session. Depending on your goals, the focus of a climbing session can range from having fun with friends to working on bouldering power or lead climbing endurance. It is a good tactic to have an idea of what you would like to accomplish in your time in the gym. Not having a plan is acceptable, just as long as you at least acknowledge that this is what you want to do. Improvements in power, endurance, or anaerobic endurance fit into the focus component of the climbing session. The focus set can also be the time to redpoint projects or push on-sight climbing skills.

Cool Down

Just as important as the warm-up, cooling down is the buffer between maximum exertion and muscle relaxation. Abruptly ending an intense climbing session by simply walking out of the gym can intensify soreness and limit recovery the following day. Stretching is ideal for cooling down, along with climbing a few easy routes. Keep in mind that the increased blood flow of aerobic activity after climbing helps flush out metabolic toxins left over from climbing. An excellent time for strength training for muscular balance is after the cool-down session.

A DELIBERATE IMPROVEMENT CYCLE

There are a multitude of training-cycle methods, all of them centered around increasing workload for a set amount of time in preparation for peak performance. The training cycle proposed here is twelve weeks long. With deliberate focus on endurance, anaerobic endurance, and power for three months, you will be prepped for maximum performance for a window of time. You can then start another training cycle at the end of the twelve-week cycle.

TWELVE-WEEK IMPROVEMENT CYCLE

WEEKS 1–3   ENDURANCE

In any physical activity, endurance is the base upon which all else is built. Since developing endurance involves a high volume of low- to moderate-intensity climbing, the occurrence of injury is less likely than in training for power. This is especially important at the beginning of a training schedule, when your body is adapting to the physical demands of training. The bulk of climbing during this three-week session is climbing at or below your on-sight grade. The more climbing done in this part of the cycle, the more fit you will be during the transitions to anaerobic endurance and power.

WEEKS 4–6   ANAEROBIC ENDURANCE

Rather than jump headfirst into high-intensity climbing after developing an adequate base of endurance, slowly add harder climbing into your training mix. If you're training for route climbing, add some bouldering sessions to change the intensity of your workouts. Alternate higher-intensity climbing sessions with endurance-oriented sessions.

WEEKS 7–9   POWER

With your foundation of endurance, mixed in with some anaerobic endurance from the last three weeks, now is the time to increase the intensity of your climbing while decreasing the volume. Because you are climbing harder routes than in the previous cycle segments, decrease the number of routes and increase the amount of rest taken between routes and climbing days.

WEEK 10   TAPERING

You have spent the past nine weeks training your body to climb better. A well-rested mind and body will improve the chances of peak performance the following week. High-intensity climbing peaked in the power-climbing segment, so decrease the intensity during the taper week, and keep the volume to a moderate level.

WEEKS 11–12   PEAK PERFORMANCE

All the hard work is done and these are the payoff weeks. This twelve-week cycle will provide at least two weeks of peak performance. If your peak-performance goal falls at the end of the cycle, be sure to extend the previous taper week to avoid prolonged inactivity.

Climbers looking for serious improvement should consider performing a physical assessment at the start of a new training cycle. Having quantifiable data on flexibility, muscular strength and endurance, and body composition is valuable in detecting improvements when taken over time (in this case, every twelve weeks). For safety and accuracy in assessment, use a personal trainer to help measure the physical components of performance.

COMPETITIONS

Most climbers say they enjoy the internal competition that climbing creates within them. That is, the body and mind have limitations, and the climber's challenge is to break those boundaries in search of self-improvement. However, with the social construct of organized competition, performance can be displayed publicly and judged against that of other athletes. Organized competitions have developed within rock climbing, serving not only as a platform of comparison but also as a celebration of the sport.

A majority of climbing competitions, or "comps," are held on artificial climbing walls with set routes. Most comps are held in gyms, but some are on walls constructed outdoors for increased spectator appeal. The routes required for competition must match the abilities of the competitors, and it is too difficult to find routes of the exact grade on real rock without scarring the environment.

While the general formats are discussed next, local and regional competitions are as unique as each gym. There are weekly adult leagues, junior team leagues, local comp series, team competitions, and even costume competitions. At the recreational level, they're all about fun, but professional climbers train just as hard and are as disciplined as any other type of professional athlete.

SPORT CLIMBING

Lead climbing competitions are also called sport climbing competitions. The first international competition was organized in the mid-1980s in Europe, where interest was strongest, and an international series followed shortly thereafter, with interest mainly in Europe. The spirit of difficulty comps was slow to gain momentum in the United States, though, as a more participant-friendly bouldering format was the norm at the regional level. But with the inclusion of climbing in the Tokyo 2020 Summer Olympic Games, sport climbing competitions have gained more momentum.

More-formal sport climbing comps call for the competitors to wait for their turn to climb in an isolation, or "iso," zone. This zone prevents the climber from seeing the routes or even from coming in contact with anyone who has. Advanced climbers almost always climb on lead, but less advanced climbers may climb on top rope. When called to climb, the climber truly makes the attempt on-sight, with no prior knowledge of the route. Each hold on the route is

worth a certain point value. The higher the hold is on the route, the greater the number of points. The climber is then scored on the highest hold reached. The attempt must be completed within a certain amount of time, but that usually does not affect the climber's performance.

A multiple-round format is popular, where to reach the final round, a climber must pass through a semifinal or even a qualifying round. Variations on difficulty comps may allow the climbers multiple attempts on routes, or the number of routes attempted by each climber may vary. More-casual, local difficulty comps may integrate bouldering or reject holding climbers in isolation to make for a more social atmosphere. Because difficulty routes require a lot of wall space, take a long time to set, and allow for only a few competitors to climb at a time, bouldering competitions are the newest wave in climbing competitions.

BOULDERING

Along with the bouldering boom of the late 1990s came bouldering comps. These competitions are merely extensions of the energy and camaraderie that have evolved within bouldering culture. Bouldering comps are run in two formats: World Cup–style and redpoint events.

World Cup–style events are molded from a more formal international format. Similar to difficulty events, climbers wait in isolation until their turn to climb. They are given a certain amount of time (around five minutes) to complete the first problem. The competitor may attempt the route as many times as desired. The highest point reached is scored, just like in a difficulty event, along with a deduction in points relative to the number of attempts. Next, the climber enters a rest period and then attempts the second problem. This true test of power and endurance is a grueling format. However, with multiple climbers attempting different routes at the same time, it makes for quite an event for spectators.

Redpoint-style bouldering competitions are popular with gyms, with hundreds of events at the local, regional, and national level held each year. To set up for a redpoint comp, the gym sets several dozen boulder problems from extremely easy to impossibly hard throughout the gym, giving each problem a point value. The more difficult the problem, the greater the point value it receives. Participants climb for several hours, attempting whichever problems they choose. Attempts and ascents are marked on a scorecard. The comp organizers determine how many problems will be scored (generally four to seven), and a climber's total score is the sum of his or her hardest problems. This format is participant-friendly, since novice climbers compete right alongside elite performers, and the atmosphere is similar to that of a high-energy bouldering session.

Opposite: *Sport climbing competitions are a test in endurance, routefinding, and power endurance.*

Bouldering competitions feature wildly dynamic movement and explosive power.

SPEED CLIMBING

The rules of a speed-climbing competition are straightforward: the fastest climber to the top wins. Two climbers compete head-to-head on identical top-rope routes. A competition may have several rounds of climbing, where the winners advance to the next round. If the climbers are not climbing on identically set routes, they may race each other twice, each having a chance on the other route, and the cumulative time will be recorded. Speed-climbing competitions are not very popular on a local level, but such events are included in international and national climbing competitions.

The aerobic demands of speed climbing are greater than that of bouldering or route climbing. Fluid, dynamic movement is essential for this fast-paced climbing, along with the ability to quickly sequence moves. A technical consideration for speed climbing is that the standard method of belaying is too slow to keep up with the slack generated from a speed climber on top rope. The belayer must modify the belay technique to reel in slack fast enough for the climber.

AN OLYMPIC SPORT

As noted, climbing will be introduced as a Summer Olympic sport in 2020. This has been a long time coming, since organized international climbing competitions started more than thirty years ago. The inclusion of climbing in the Olympics will change the landscape of the sport. For one, the Olympic format will consist of all three disciplines of climbing: speed, sport, and bouldering. Currently, most climbers specialize and focus on one, or maybe two, of the disciplines, but the new format celebrates the most well-rounded competition climbers. Climbers now have the chance to be Olympians, and the sport of climbing is now held in the highest echelon of sports competitions, commanding the same respect as track and field, gymnastics, or swimming. To go along with that, the stakes of climbing competitions are now higher. More time, effort, money, and research will be put into all aspects of climbing performance. It's certain that the boundaries of the four pillars of performance discussed in this chapter—technical skill, mental approach, physical conditioning, and scheduling and periodization—will be pushed in the coming years in preparation for climbing's Olympic debut.

Because climbing will soon be an Olympic sport, expect to see a significant progression of talent over the next few years. These climbers are the winners of the 2016 Bouldering World Cup in Vail, Colorado.

MAINTAINING BALANCE

The best step to staying healthy is avoiding injury. When you do sustain a climbing injury, seek professional assistance for prompt rehabilitation. Also remember that your health depends on more than simply avoiding injury. While injury impedes climbing progress, staying healthy is the platform that allows for climbing improvement, and maintaining physical fitness and listening to your body will help you cope with stress and fight illness. Take the following measures into consideration to help maintain health and avoid injury.

AVOID OVERTRAINING

When training for climbing performance, high-intensity workouts can decrease performance for the following twelve to thirty-six hours, depending on the intensity. This is a natural reaction, as your body goes through a recovery cycle from the beating it just endured. If you do not allow enough rest between each training bout, then your body can never fully recover. Symptoms of overtraining can include a constant sense of fatigue, a general feeling of heaviness, or even loss of appetite.

LISTEN TO YOUR BODY

Whoever came up with the saying "Pain is only weakness leaving the body" probably did not get very far. Pain is the body's way of telling you that something is wrong and needs to be addressed. Even nagging discomfort, in a finger tendon or an elbow, will not go away on its own. Of course, the immediate remedy for pain is to stop performing the action that aggravates the injury.

But from there, climbers need to not only listen to their bodies but also help them recover. Even minor discomforts can escalate to debilitating pain, so get checked out by a doctor if rest does not significantly improve the problem. Do not climb through pain. You will only make your injury worse. Also, keep in mind that climbing to exhaustion increases the risk of injury, since weak muscles lose their ability to stabilize the body.

Properly Fuel and Hydrate

High-energy climbing sessions are often fueled by excitement and fun (and perhaps vast quantities of caffeine), rather than by food and water. If you are hitting the gym after work, eat something before or during your climbing session. If you do not, your body simply will not be able to keep up with your demands. Hydration is another issue gym climbers tend to overlook. If you climb while dehydrated, the risk of injury and muscle cramping increases. In a two-hour climbing session, drink at least one quart of water.

Gradual Reentry

Taking a break from climbing for one to several weeks can rejuvenate your body and refresh your mind, but the longer the break, the more susceptible you are to injury upon reentry. While climbing-movement skills may not be affected by the hiatus, muscle and tendon strength, along with joint range of motion, will have decreased. When you're reentering the sport, the difference between what your mind tells your body to do and what it can handle can result in injury. After any break, gradually increase the intensity of your climbing. It is impractical to expect to pick up where you left off.

Evaluate High-Risk Moves

Harder climbs can require new body movement. High-risk moves, like shallow finger pockets, high gastons, or severe drop-knee moves, should be performed with caution. Listening to your body and falling at the first sense of potential injury is the better alternative to doing the move and blowing out your knee.

NONCLIMBING ACTIVITIES

Nonclimbing activities that work on the flexibility, muscular strength, and stability required for climbing can improve climbing performance. For instance, dancing can improve dynamic balance and can even provide an aerobic workout. Gymnastics requires similar muscular demands as climbing. Pilates focuses on core body strength. Yoga improves flexibility, postural alignment, total body muscular stability, and even mental grounding. Because of the similar physical and mental demands and benefits of yoga and climbing, it is common for gyms to offer yoga classes. By engaging in physical activities other than climbing, your mind and body remain balanced against any rigors encountered.

PUTTING IT ALL TOGETHER

A multitude of factors contribute to climbing improvement. From the partners you choose to how much stretching you do before a climb, and from the hangboard workouts to aerobic training, it all makes a difference. An eager climber may want to overhaul his current climbing routine and change every aspect. But changing too many aspects of the activity can alter the initial experience, and the allure of climbing is no longer the same. Also, it is difficult to determine which of the variables actually made the difference in performance.

If you desire to improve your climbing by taking steps to higher performance, change your approach one aspect at a time. Climbing three times a week for three hours per session *and* doing aerobic exercise five times a week for a half hour each workout *and* strength training two times a week *and* a structured yoga class every week will leave you no time to enjoy the other things in life and will almost guarantee injury and fatigue.

Start by improving the aspect of climbing that is your weakest link. For some people, that may mean going back to the basics of movement technique, or for others, improving endurance. Do not allow training to cause you to lose sight of why you climb. If what you are doing is not fun, then perhaps you should reconsider your goals. If you are not enjoying the activity, then what is the point?

BEYOND THE GYM

Gym climbing is a fulfilling activity in itself. With so many climbing gyms and new climbers every year, it's becoming more mainstream than its predecessor—rock climbing outside on real rock. Anyone who enjoys gym climbing has surely thought about breaking out of the artificial holds and manmade walls of the gym to climb outside. If that appeals to you, there are some extremely important factors to consider before heading out to your local crag.

While your indoor skills will translate somewhat to climbing on rock, they're not enough for you to start leading sport routes up cliffs like this climber without proper mentorship or guidance. (Photo by Matt Burbach)

Mastering the skills in this book, or being a 5.13 gym climber or competition climber, does *not* prepare you for climbing outdoors.

A SHARED ENVIRONMENT

The gym is a controlled environment, and climbing outside simply isn't. Climbers often share their activity with others who enjoy the same landscape, such as hikers, mountain bikers, and other outdoor enthusiasts. Seldom are climbers the only users of an area, particularly when you consider the natural wildlife and landscape. We are guests outside, and it's a privilege for us to be able to climb. There are no trash cans, toilets, recycling bins, and couches at most outdoor climbing destinations, and it's essential to practice a Leave No Trace policy. The Access Fund, a nonprofit organization that protects climbing areas in the United States, has developed a pact to promote responsible outdoor climbing etiquette. Commit to the pact:

1. Be considerate of other users.
2. Park and camp in designated areas.
3. Dispose of human waste properly.
4. Stay on trails whenever possible.
5. Place gear and pads on durable surfaces.

6. Respect wildlife, sensitive plants, soils, and cultural references.
7. Clean up chalk and tick marks.
8. Minimize group size and noise.
9. Pack out all trash, crash pads, and gear.
10. Learn the local ethics for the places you climb.
11. Respect regulations and closures.
12. Use, install, and replace bolts and fixed anchors responsibly.
13. Be an upstander, not a bystander.

CLIMBING ON ROCK

Transitioning to the outdoors isn't always particularly smooth. In fact, the more seasoned you are at gym climbing, the more trouble you may have adjusting to real rock. For instance, everything is "on route." There obviously are no colored holds to give you any direction, and a route setter has not designed a series of fluid moves. You're on your own. And the gym is limited to bolt-on holds with manmade texture. Outdoors, you get what the natural features give you. From smooth, polished limestone footholds to grippy granite slopers, the possibilities are infinite. There isn't really a substitute for climbing on real rock. So be patient, and don't expect to immediately climb the same grades outside as you would in the gym.

KNOWLEDGE OF RISK AND RESPONSIBILITY

Outside, on real rock, there are no top ropes hanging from rock walls or boulder fields lined with padded flooring. You have to set up top-rope anchors yourself, bring and position your own crash pads, or place your own trad or sport climbing gear. There's no instructor or staff person, and the consequences can be severe. One of the most important skills for climbing outside is being able to assess the risks your situation poses. Are you able to assess whether or not the bolts are in good condition? How about protecting yourself from a rocky landing for a boulder problem? Or the possible consequences of a fall while leading above a ledge?

SAFETY SYSTEMS

Possessing all the required gym climbing equipment is not sufficient for climbing outside. The safety systems, even for bouldering, are different outside than they are in the gym. Not only do you need the equipment and gear but, more importantly, you must acquire the technical knowledge to safely use that equipment. Climbing outside is a bad time for trial and error.

A STARTING POINT

Pointing out these differences between indoor and outdoor climbing emphasizes the need for comprehensive learning and knowledge before heading outside. The best climbing gyms are those that create communities that promote and share their passion for climbing—not just in the gym. Many gyms have or partner with rock climbing guide services to help gym climbers make the transition from gym to crag. If you're lucky enough to have climbing areas nearby, group day classes are a good introduction, and private guiding can be catered to your individual needs.

Whether or not they offer outdoor instruction, gyms are community hubs to meet and share new experiences with other climbers. Before you partner up with someone and head out to the crag, it's imperative for you to understand that person's experience. The fact that he hasn't had any accidents may mean he's lucky—not safe. Going with a group, particularly a mix of familiar and unfamiliar faces, is a good idea, so that people can share their knowledge and experience.

Acknowledgments

More than twenty years ago, I was inspired when I opened up an outdoor equipment catalog to a photo of Yuji Hirayama climbing in Yosemite. I thought to myself, "That's what I want to do when I grow up." I immediately sought out a local climbing gym and engrossed myself in the activity and lifestyle of climbing. My journey as a climber has been long, adventurous, humbling, and fulfilling.

Special thanks go out to Chris Warner and Earth Treks Climbing Centers. For more than two decades, Earth Treks Climbing Centers have been at the forefront of the gym climbing experience, continually driving evolution in the industry, and more importantly, the community, transforming the gym climbing lifestyle into what it is and what it will become. My experience at Earth Treks set the foundation of my career in the climbing and outdoor industry, for which I'm incredibly grateful. I'd like to thank the climbing community as a whole. It's made up of so many unique characters—the strongest bonds I've formed in life have been through the experience of climbing.

Resources

These organizations and news outlets are key resources for climbers.

American Alpine Club
https://americanalpineclub.org
The AAC is the authority of climbing information and knowledge. They've been working very hard to standardize best practices in all aspects of climbing, including gym belay certification and education.

Access Fund
www.accessfund.org
Access Fund's mission is to protect climbing access and the integrity of America's outdoor climbing areas. They also provide education on minimizing climbers' impact in the environment. Every climber should support Access Fund.

Climbing Business Journal
www.climbingbusinessjournal.com
The CBJ is more than an independent news outlet dedicated to covering the indoor climbing industry. They also have the latest news of industry practices, climbing competitions, youth coaching, route setting, and the most comprehensive, up-to-date interactive gym listing online.

The Mountaineers
www.mountaineers.org
Based in the Pacific Northwest, The Mountaineers have been helping people explore, conserve, learn about, and enjoy local lands and beyond since the early twentieth century. Their comprehensive outdoor climbing education program extends from gym and rock climbing to alpinism and mountaineering.

Mountain Project
www.mountainproject.com
This online reference is the definitive source and guide for climbing. Their route guides are extensive, with up-to-date news feeds, articles, and gym references. Their forums cover a wide range of climbing topics.

Glossary

aerobic exercise Cardiovascular activity, such as running, swimming, or biking.

anaerobic endurance The ability to generate strength multiple times. Also known as *power endurance*.

arête Outside corner feature of a climbing surface.

assisted-braking belay device A belay device that provides supplementary braking power. See also *GriGri*.

auto-belay Indoor top-rope belay method that employs a mechanical device to take in slack as the climber ascends and automatically lower the climber to the ground after she comes off the wall.

back-clipped An incorrectly clipped quickdraw that can potentially unclip if the rope runs over it in a fall.

back-stepping the rope Allowing the rope to trail behind the leg or foot while lead climbing, which creates the potential for inverting the climber in the event of a fall.

barn door An off-balance body position that causes a foot, hand, or both to rotate away from the wall.

belay anchor Attachment point used to secure the belayer to the ground. See also *floor anchor*.

belay device Piece of equipment used by the belayer to increase the running friction of the rope and to keep the climber safe.

belay gloves Close-fitting leather gloves that give the belayer an added layer of protection from the rope.

belay loop Nylon loop of webbing that attaches to the waist belt and leg loops of the harness.

"Belay on" Belayer's response to the climber confirming that the belayer is ready to belay.

belay stance The belayer's body positioning. An athletic stance with one foot slightly in front of the other and knees bent, ready to absorb the force of the climber's fall.

belay test Competency test that each gym gives to climbers to ensure proper belay skills.

belayer The person who manages the rope for the climber and keeps the rope from moving in the event of a fall.

belayer's neck Neck soreness from looking up at the climber while belaying.

"Belay's off" Belayer's acknowledgment that he is not belaying the climber anymore.

bent-gate carabiners Carabiners with a curved gate to make clipping the rope easier.

beta Information or instruction for a climb. Derived from "beta-max" video, when climbers started to use video analysis to review their movement.

bicycle move One foot pushes against a hold while the other foot toe hooks the same hold to stabilize the body. This move is often performed on steep terrain or roofs.

bight Loop of rope.

bouldering Climbing unroped on boulders or traversing low to the ground. Often associated with very difficult, short bursts of climbing.

bouldering pad Large pad used to cushion the impact of a boulderer's fall. Also called a *crash pad.*

brake hand The hand used to brake the climber in the event of a fall. The brake hand is always in contact with the brake strand and is usually the belayer's dominant hand.

brake position Positioning the brake hand below the belay device with a firm grip to keep the rope from moving.

brake strand End of the rope that extends from the belay device and is held by the belayer's brake hand.

campus board A training board with wooden rungs for footless upper-body training.

campusing Training or climbing without the use of feet. Often in reference to a campus board.

carabiner Aluminum or steel clip with a spring-loaded gate. Carabiners are used to attach climbing equipment and ropes together.

chalk bag Hand-sized bag that is filled with gymnastics chalk, which serves as a drying element for the hands. The bag attaches to the harness or a belt.

chalk ball Mesh ball filled with chalk. Some gyms allow only chalk balls in order to minimize the amount of loose chalk dust indoors.

"Climb on" Confirmation from the belayer to the climber that the climber is ascending.

"Climbing" Spoken by the climber to let the belayer know that she is about to climb.

core The middle structure of a climbing rope composed of tiny filaments, providing the elastic properties of the rope.

crash pad See *bouldering pad.*

crimping Grabbing an edge with the hands by placing the fingertips on the hold and buckling the knuckles under the pressure of weighting the hold.

crossing through Moving the hands or feet across the body to minimize frontal positioning.

crux The hardest part of a climb or boulder problem.

deadpoint The point where a climber's center of gravity is motionless during a dynamic move, just after moving up and before coming back down. Deadpoint moves are momentum-based movement where the climber reaches for a hold at the height of his center of gravity.

difficulty comps Events in which winning is based on how high or far the climbers ascend. These competitions are either top-rope or sport climbing.

dihedral The inside of a corner.

doubled back The final stage of securing a harness buckle in which half of the buckle is covered with webbing.

draw See *quickdraw*.

dressing Configuring a knot to minimize rope twists or to adjust segment lengths.

drop knee Rotating the knee toward the midline to help rotate the hips and twist the body.

dynamic movement Momentum-based movement often generated by the climber's center of gravity.

dyno Dynamic movement. Often used to describe extremely long moves in which the hands and feet lose contact with the wall.

edging Stepping on a hold using the edge of the foot.

external imagery Visualization based on viewing yourself as if someone were filming you and you were watching the results on a monitor.

"Falling" Spoken by a climber to let the belayer know he is falling.

feeding rope When the belayer gives out slack to the climber.

figure-eight follow-through An easy-to-identify knot commonly used by the climber to tie in to the rope. Also called a *figure-eight retrace*.

figure-eight retrace See *figure-eight follow-through*.

fingerlock Placing the fingertips into a crack and rotating the entire hand to lock the fingers in the crack.

flagging Placing the inside or outside edge of the foot against the wall for stability.

flake To lay down or loosely stack a rope so that the climber's end is on top. This prevents tangles as the rope is pulled off the ground.

flash pump An overaccumulation of lactic acid from not properly warming up.

floor anchor Ground attachment point in climbing gyms to keep the belayer affixed to the floor. See also *belay anchor*.

flow The ability to string multiple, uninterrupted moves together.

foot jam Sliding the foot into a crack as far as it will go and rotating the knee so it points straight up and the foot turns down, securing the hold. See also *toe jam*.

frontal position A climbing stance in which the shoulders and hips are square, with the center of gravity close to the wall. The inside edges of the feet are used and the knees are turned out.

gaston A type of "pushing" sidepull where the positive part of the hold is facing the climber.

gate The moving part of a carabiner that opens and shuts.

gear loops Plastic or nylon loops attached to a harness's waist belt, used for clipping carabiners and gear.

grade Describes a route or boulder problem's difficulty. In indoor climbing, interchangeable with *rating*.

GriGri Assisted-braking belay device that is popular among gym and sport climbers.

guide hand The belayer's free hand, or the one not used for braking.

gym climbing Indoor climbing on an artificial climbing wall.

hand jam Placing the entire hand into a crack and squeezing the hand to allow it to expand and stay placed.

hangboard Shoulder-width wall-mounted device with multiple hand grips used for developing hand and upper-body conditioning. Also called a *fingerboard*.

harness Padded webbing seat used to attach the climber or belayer to the rope or other safety anchors. Also used for attaching climbing gear.

heel hook Placing the heel of the foot on top or around a foothold to pull the hips in over the hold.

high-step Placing the foot high up the wall, often requiring the stepping knee to be turned out to keep the hips close to the wall.

ice climbing Form of roped climbing in which climbers ascend ice features, such as frozen waterfalls.

internal imagery Visualization from the perspective of seeing your environment as if you were on the route.

International Climbing and Mountaineering Federation See *UIAA*.

jug A large, comfortable incut or handlebar hold.

lace-up shoes Climbing shoes with a traditional lacing system that extends down to the toe rand. These shoes offer the most adjustment of fit.

last Shaped footprint of a climbing shoe.

lead anchors Final anchors of a lead climb that the leader must clip the rope through to be lowered.

lead climbing Form of roped climbing in which the climber's rope trails down to the belayer below. The climber periodically attaches the rope to pieces of protective gear fixed to the rock or wall.

leg loops Leg straps that are a part of the harness and that fit on the upper thigh. Some are adjustable.

"Lower" Spoken by the climber to let the belayer know that she wants to be lowered.

mantling Pushing down on the top of a boulder or ledge until your hips are high enough to step up next to your hands.

matching Placing either both hands or both feet on the same hold.

muscular balance Having a proportionally appropriate amount of strength between climbing-specific and seldom-used muscles. Muscular imbalance can lead to injury.

muscular endurance The ability to generate strength multiple times.

muscular strength Amount of force generated by a muscle or group of muscles.

"Off belay" What the climber says after he is back on the ground and no longer in need of a belayer.

"On belay" Spoken by the climber to confirm that the belayer is ready to protect the climber.

on-sight To climb a route from start to finish without falling or weighting the rope and without any prior knowledge of the route, including watching others.

open hand Grabbing a hold using a relaxed hand grip, in which the fingers are fairly straight.

overhang A face that leans toward the climber, forcing the climber to put more weight on her upper body.

periodization Variations in the intensity, duration, mode, and frequency of training.

pinching Using the thumb to squeeze the entire hand while grabbing a hold.

pocket A hold with an indentation in which the fingers or the toes fit.

power Amount of work performed divided by the amount of time it takes to perform the work.

power endurance See *anaerobic endurance*.

problem A bouldering route.

quickdraw Two carabiners attached to one another by a piece of nylon webbing, used to clip in to on sport climbs. Also called a *draw*.

rand Thin rubber extending above the sole of the climbing shoe. The toe rand can be replaced.

rating Numerical system describing a route or boulder problem's difficulty. Also called *grade* in indoor climbing; see also *Yosemite Decimal System* and *V scale*.

redpoint ascent Completing a route without falling or weighting the rope, having already made a first attempt.

resole The process of replacing the worn-down sole of a climbing shoe with a new sole.

rise Distance between the harness's waist belt and leg loops.

roof Severely overhanging to horizontal feature that must be climbed from the underside.

route setter Person who positions holds on a climbing wall to design a route or a boulder problem.

sequencing Determining where to go, which hand- and footholds to use, and proper body positioning on a climb.

setting a knot Tightening a knot by hand immediately after tying it in order to minimize knot slippage at a later time.

sharp end The lead climber's end of the rope.

sheath Loosely woven protective casing surrounding a climbing rope's core.

sidepull A sideways-positioned handhold that requires the climber to lean away from the hold to create enough opposition for stability.

slab Less-than-vertical climbing terrain.

"Slack" Command used when the climber needs more rope from the belayer.

slip-lasted Describes a climbing shoe constructed with a sensitive last slipped in.

slippers Laceless climbing shoes that offer the most sensitivity. They must be sized extremely tight to minimize the foot sliding around inside.

sloper A hold that slopes down and away from the wall and is often difficult to hold on to.

smearing Positioning the sole of the foot against the wall by lowering the heel to increase the surface area and pressure between the sole and wall.

speed-climbing competitions Competitions in which the winner is the climber who ascends the fastest. These are top-rope events.

sport climbing Form of lead climbing in which the climber attaches the rope to fixed bolts and anchors on the rock or wall. All gym lead climbing is sport climbing.

static movement In-control movement sustained by the climber's muscles. A good indication of static movement is whether or not the climber can stop at any point during the move.

stemming Pushing the hands or feet in opposition, often in a corner.

straight-gate carabiners Carabiners with a traditionally straight gate. A multiuse carabiner.

system wall Training wall with mirrored holds positioned left and right of center, often with adjustable steepness.

tail Amount of rope that extends from a knot to the end of the rope.

"Take" Climber's command telling the belayer to take the climber's weight on the rope.

test piece Climb or boulder problem that represents a significant difficulty or achievement.

toe hook Using the top part of the foot or toes to hook around a foothold. Often used on steep, overhanging terrain.

toe jam Inserting the toes into a crack and turning the foot down to lock the toes in place, securing the hold. See also *foot jam*.

top rope A roped climbing system in which the climbing rope travels up to an anchor at the top of the route and then back down to the belayer.

tracking Climbing indoors using only the hand- and footholds that are designated as a part of the route being attempted.

trad climbing Form of roped climbing in which lead climber places pieces of protection to which she secures the rope.

traversing Horizontal climbing often done close to the ground and without a rope.

tubular belay device A generally lightweight, manually locking belay device that a majority of climbers use for belaying.

twistlocking Twisting the hips and body and ultimately locking the arm to allow the reaching arm to extend.

UIAA Union Internationale des Associations d'Alpinisme, or International Climbing and Mountaineering Federation. International organization governing the safety standards of climbing gear.

undercling Handhold that is grabbed on the bottom, with the reaching hand's palm facing the climber.

"Up rope" Spoken by the climber to the belayer, announcing that slack needs to be taken up.

Velcro shoes Climbing shoes with Velcro closures. Easy to put on and take off, and they allow fit adjustments.

visualization Mental imagery of climbing performance.

V scale Bouldering rating scale ranging from V0 to V17.

waist belt Uppermost part of the harness that snugly fits around the smallest part of the waist.

waiver of liability Legal agreement that must be signed by the participant (or a parent or legal guardian if the participant is a minor) acknowledging the risks of climbing indoors.

webbing Usually nylon, woven flat like a strap or belt. Often used in harnesses, nylon quickdraws, and belay anchors.

weight shifting Controlling the center of gravity to properly keep weight over the legs and feet.

wire-gate carabiners Carabiners with gates made of looped wire, for lighter weight and less movement.

Yosemite Decimal System (YDS) Rating system for climbing routes. All indoor, roped climbing routes have a prefix of 5 and the number after the decimal designates the difficulty from 1 to 15. Climbs higher than 5.10 may be further categorized with *a* through *d*.

Z clip Incorrect clipping of quickdraws that results when quickdraws are clipped in the incorrect order, forcing the rope into a Z-shaped line and creating tremendous rope drag.

Index

A

aerobic exercise, 193

anaerobic endurance, 192, 196

anchoring

belayer, 151–52

    description of, 125–26

    arm stretch, 176

assisted-braking belay devices, 42–43, 156, 158–59

auto-belay systems, 131–32

B

belay devices, 42–45. *See also* Petzl GriGri; tubular belay devices

belay gloves, 47

belay loop, 38

belay test, 26–27

belayer

    anchoring of, 151–52

    positioning of, 152

    safety check of, 129

belaying

    with assisted-braking belay devices, 156, 158–59

    auto-belay systems, 131–32

    commands during, 126–27

exercises for, 130–31, 158–59, 161

lead climbing, 135, 151–64

motion of, 153–59

with Petzl GriGri, 121–25, 156–57, 157

rope management preclimb, 152–53

safety check before, 129

safety during, 159–60

top-rope, 116–26, 132

with tubular belay device, 116–21, 154–55

unanchored, 152

biceps stretch, 176

blindfolded climbing exercise, 69

body composition, 192–93, 197

body positioning, 63–66, 144–45

body tension, 98–99

bouldering

    advanced techniques for, 98–108

    body tension, 98–99

    competitions in, 199–200

    descend from, 93

    description of, 19, 88–89

    falling while, 93–95

    finishing, 91–92

    following a problem, 91–93

    getting started, 89–91

mantling, 104–05
movement during, 106–08
for power, 187–89
safety during, 91, 108
spotting during, 95–98, 108
V scale, 90–91
bouldering pads, 95
bowline, 137
brake position, 117, 156
buckles, 37–38

C
campus board, 190–91
carabiners
definition of, 40
for lead climbing, 136
locking, 40–41
nonlocking, 40
safety check of, 129
shape of, 41
strength of, 41–42
chalk, 45–46
chalk bag, 46
chest
strength conditioning of, 180
stretching of, 176
climbers, 53–54, 136
climbing
description of, 16–18
etiquette for, 204–05
by feel, 69
lead. *See* lead climbing
on-rock, 205
for power, 187–89
top-rope. *See* top-rope climbing
warming up before, 194–95
with your legs, 64
climbing gyms, 18–25, 27, 48–49

climbing shoes, 30–36
climbing walls, 18
clipping the rope, 138–42, 146–47
clothing, 47–48
communication, commands, 126–27, 138
community centers, 25
competitions, 197–201
conditioning
hand strength, 185–87
hangboard, 183–87
muscular, 178–79
physical, 174
upper-body, 184–85
cool down, 195
core strength, 98, 180–83
costs, 27
crimping, 67
crossing through, 75–79

D
dead hangs, 185–87
deadpoints, 80–81
dips, 180
drop-knee moves, 101–02
dynamic movement, 53, 80–84
dynos, 81–84

E
edges, 66–68
edging, 58
endurance, 191–92, 196
entry fees, 27
environment, 204–05
equipment
belay devices, 42–45. *See also* Petzl GriGri;
tubular belay devices
belay gloves, 47
carabiners. *See* carabiners

caring for, 43
chalk, chalk bag, 45–46
harness, 37–40
helmet, 47
lead climbing, 135–36
purchasing of, 48–50
rope, 43–45. *See also* rope
shoes, 30–36
standards and testing of, 50
used, 49–50

F
falling
  in bouldering, 93–95
  in lead climbing, 149–50
fat, body, 193
figure eight follow–through,
  112–14
finger stretch, 176–77
fingerlocks, 70
fitness centers, 24–25
flagging, 60–61
flexibility, 175, 197
floor anchor, 151
focus set, 195
following a problem, 91–93
foot exchanges, 70–75
foot jams, 60
foot roll match, 72–73
footwork
  edging, 58
  exercises for, 62
  flagging, 60–61
  foot jams, 60
  heel hooks, 59–60
  high-steps, 63
  pockets, 58–59
  smearing, 59, 75

stemming, 63
toe hooks, 59–60
toe jams, 60
forearm "flash pump," 194
forearm stretch, 176–77

G
gaston, 66
gear. *See* equipment
gear loop, 38
gloves, 47
good-hold/bad-hold exercise, 78
grade of climb, 111–12
ground fall zone, 147
ground-up sequencing, 84
gyms, 16–25, 27, 48–49, 203, 205

H
hamstrings stretch, 178
hand(s)
  strength conditioning for, 185–87
  stretches for, 176–77
hand jams, 70
hand/foot pause exercise, 72
hangboard conditioning, 183–87
harness, 37–40
health, 201–02
heel hooks, 59–60, 103–04
helmet, 47
high-risk moves, 202–03
high-steps, 63
hips stretch, 177–78
hop-step, 72, 75
hydration, 202

I
in-climb sequencing, 84
indoor climbing, 16–18, 22–25

instruction, 22–23
introductory class, 26

K
kettlebell Russian twist, 182
knot
    dressing and setting of, 114–16
    figure eight follow-through, 112–14

L
lateral movements, 76
lead anchors, 150
lead climbing
    belaying, 135, 151–64
    body positioning during, 144–45
    clipping the rope for, 138–42
    commands during, 138
    communication during, 137–38
    description of, 20–21, 134–35
    falling during, 149–50
    gear for, 135–36
    ground fall zone during, 147
    lead anchors for, 150
    rope management during,
        147–48
    route selection, 136–37,
        163–64
    safety check before, 137
    techniques of, 136
    tying in for, 137
    Z-clip for, 142–44
Leave No Trace, 204
leg climbing, 64
leg loops, 38
liability waiver, 27
liquid chalk, 46
locking carabiners, 40–41
lock-offs, 184

lowering of climber
    with Petzl GriGri, 124–25
    with tubular belay device, 120–21
low-hands climbing, 64

M
mantling, 104–05
matching hands and feet, 70–75
middle-finger grab technique, 141–42
Moon Boards, 190–91
movement
    body positioning, 63–66
    during bouldering, 106–08
    crossing through, 75–79
    deadpoints, 80–81
    dynamic, 53, 80–84
    dynos, 81–84
    footwork, 58–63
    hand grips for, 66–70
    lateral, 76
    matching hands and feet, 70–75
    practicing of, 53
    sequencing, 85–86
    static, 53
    types of, 52–53
    weight shifting, 54–58
muscular balance, 179–83
muscular strength, 178–79, 187, 191, 197

N
neck stretch, 178
nonclimbing activities, 203
nonlocking carabiners, 40

O
Olympic sport, 201
open hand grip, 67–68
overtraining, 202

P

pain, 202

periodization, 193–97

Petzl GriGri

    belaying with, 121–25, 156–57, 157

    description of, 43

    setting up, 121–22

physical conditioning, 174

pinch technique, 142

pinching, 68

plank, 181

pockets

    foot position in, 58–59

    hand grip in, 68

power, 187–89, 196

preclimb sequence, 84

pull-up, 184–85

push-ups, 180

Q

quickdraw, 141–42, 146

quiet feet and stare-down exercise, 62

R

rear keeper straps, 38

rope

    clipping the, 138–42, 146–47

    description of, 43–45

    during lead climbing, 147–48

    unclipping the, 142

route

    identifying of, 112

    lead climbing, 136–37, 163–64

    setting of, 21–22

route-climbing competitions, 198–99

Russian twist, 181–82

S

safety, 205

    during bouldering, 91, 108

    during lead climbing, 137

    during top-rope climbing, 129

scheduling, 193–97

screw lock, 40

sequencing, 84–86

shoes, 30–36

shoulder stretch, 175–76

sidepull, 66

skill refinement, 195

slack, 118–20, 124, 154, 156

slopers, 70

smearing, 59, 75

speed climbing, 200

sport climbing, 197–99

spotting, 95–98, 108

stance, 54

static movement, 53

stemming, 63

straight-on body position, 63–64

strength

    climbing-specific, 183–84

    hand, 185–87

    muscular, 178–79, 187, 191, 197

stretching, 175–78

system wall, 189–91

T

tapering, 196

technique refinement, 195

terrain, 111–12

toe hooks, 59–60, 104

toe jams, 60

top-rope climbing

belaying, 116–26, 132

communication, commands during, 126–27

description of, 20, 109–10

grade for, 111–12

illustration of, 20

safety checks, 129

tying in, 112–16

training cycles, 195–97

training walls

campus board, 190–91

for climbing power, 187–91

description of, 184

for endurance, 187, 191–92

system wall, 189–91

triceps

strength conditioning of, 180–81

stretching of, 177

tubular belay devices

belaying with, 116–21, 154–55

description of, 42

setting up, 116–17

twistlocks, 99–101

twist, stretch, 178

tying in, 112–16, 137

typewriter pull–ups, 185

U

undercling, 64–66

upper back stretch, 175–76

upper-body conditioning, 184–85

used equipment, 49–50

V

V scale, 90–91, 112

W

waist belt, 37–38

waiver of liability, 27

warming up, 194–95

websites, 48

weight shifting

center of gravity, 55

description of, 54–55

exercises for, 56–57

foot precision in, 58

stance width and, 54

Y

yoga classes, 23

Yosemite Decimal System, 22, 90, 111–12

youth teams and programs, 23–24

Z

Z-clip, 142–44

About the Author

Jon Glassberg

More than two decades ago, **Matt Burbach's** first experience climbing was in a climbing gym. In that time, he has dedicated his career to sharing his passion for climbing. Matt completed his bachelor of science in exercise science and kinesiology at the University of Maryland while writing his first climbing book for Mountaineers Books and serving as a climbing instructor and coach. Upon the book's publication, he became the founding editor of *Urban Climber Magazine*, the first— and only—magazine devoted to bouldering, gym, sport, and competition climbing. Over the past decade, Matt has continued to share his passion for climbing by focusing on creating brand experiences for major outdoor and climbing industry brands.

About the Photographer

Jon Glassberg spent the first two decades of his life as a pro climber, traveling the world, climbing rocks, and generally getting after it. While Jon climbs 5.14 and V14 to this day, his focus has shifted from the rock to the camera, with an emphasis on directing, refined from his simple climbing beginnings and authentic view on the outdoor industry and action sports. His dedication and consistency have allowed him to capture the heart and soul of cutting-edge climbing while growing his company, Louder Than Eleven, into one of the outdoor industry's most trusted production houses. Jon has a rare insider's path, which allows him to work with the pros on their level, go places few others are willing to go, and capture authentic, high-quality commercial images in both the vertical and horizontal worlds. Jon enjoys hanging from the side of El Capitan capturing free ascents 3000 feet off the valley floor, climbing in the Rocky Mountains, and traveling to the corners of the earth to capture rare moments in sport.

Louder Than Eleven

MOUNTAINEERS BOOKS

SKIPSTONE   BRAIDED RIVER

recreation · lifestyle · conservation

MOUNTAINEERS BOOKS, including its two imprints, Skipstone and Braided River, is a leading publisher of quality outdoor recreation, sustainability, and conservation titles. As a 501(c)(3) nonprofit, we are committed to supporting the environmental and educational goals of our organization by providing expert information on human-powered adventure, sustainable practices at home and on the trail, and preservation of wilderness.

Our publications are made possible through the generosity of donors, and through sales of more than 800 titles on outdoor recreation, sustainable lifestyle, and conservation. To donate, purchase books, or learn more, visit us online:

MOUNTAINEERS BOOKS
1001 SW Klickitat Way, Suite 201 • Seattle, WA 98134
800-553-4453 • mbooks@mountaineersbooks.org • www.mountaineersbooks.org

Leave No Trace strives to educate visitors about the nature of their recreational impacts and offers techniques to prevent and minimize such impacts. • Leave No Trace is best understood as an educational and ethical program, not as a set of rules and regulations • For more information, visit www.lnt.org or call 800-332-4100.

OTHER TITLES YOU MIGHT ENJOY FROM MOUNTAINEERS BOOKS